W9-AFD-715

SIR EDWIN LUTYENS

DESIGNING IN THE ENGLISH TRADITION

Learning Resources Center
Carroll Community College
1601 Washington Rd.
Westminster, MD 21157

WITHDRAWN

SIR EDWIN LUTYENS

DESIGNING IN THE ENGLISH TRADITION

BY ELIZABETH WILHIDE
FOREWORD BY CANDIA LUTYENS

HARRY N. ABRAMS, INC., PUBLISHERS

TO M.L.

DESIGNED BY NIGEL PARTRIDGE

LIBRARY OF CONGRESS CATALOGING-IN-PUBLICATION DATA

WILHIDE, ELIZABETH.

SIR EDWIN LUTYENS: DESIGNING IN THE ENGLISH TRADITION / BY ELIZABETH WILHIDE;

FOREWORD BY CANDIA LUTYENS

P. CM.

INCLUDES BIBLIOGRAPHIC REFERENCES AND INDEX.

ISBN 0–8109–4080–9 (HC)

1. LUTYENS, EDWIN LANDSEER, SIR, 1869–1944 — CRITICISM AND INTERPRETATION. 2.

ARCHITECTURE, DOMESTIC — ENGLAND. 3. ARCHITECTURE, MODERN —20TH CENTURY — ENGLAND 4.

INTERIOR DECORATION — ENGLAND — HISTORY — 20TH CENTURY. 5. ARCHITECTS — ENGLAND — BIOGRAPHY.

I. TITLE

NA997. L8 W55 2000

720.92 — dc21   00-28033

TEXT © 2000 ELIZABETH WILHIDE

DESIGN AND LAYOUT © 2000 PAVILION BOOKS LTD.

FIRST PUBLISHED IN GREAT BRITAIN IN 2000 BY

PAVILION BOOKS LIMITED, LONDON

PUBLISHED IN 2000 BY HARRY N. ABRAMS, INCORPORATED, NEW YORK

ALL RIGHTS RESERVED. NO PART OF THE CONTENTS OF THIS BOOK MAY BE REPRODUCED WITHOUT THE WRITTEN PERMISSION OF THE PUBLISHER

PRINTED AND BOUND IN SINGAPORE

HARRY N. ABRAMS, INC.

100 FIFTH AVENUE

NEW YORK, N.Y. 10011

www.abramsbooks.com

FRONTISPIECE: *The gateway at Orchards.*

RIGHT: *Caricature of Lutyens smoking a pipe*

and wearing a solar topee.

CONTENTS

CONTENTS

FOREWORD

—

*'Buildings are among the most enduring and unequivocal records of
the past as well as being memorials to those who build and live in
them and buildings are those facts of history with which we are in the
most continual contact throughout our lives.'*

So wrote my father, Robert Lutyens, only son of Sir Edwin, by way of an introduction to his book *Six Great Architects* in 1958. He wrote at a time when the architecture of Lutyens was vilified, subsumed by the Modern Movement and deemed irrelevant to the post-war utopia of modern estates and servantless living. Nevertheless, that his father was one of the six was no act of filial bias but a statement of the obvious. That amongst British architects defined as great, Lutyens should share the laurels with Jones, Wren, Adam, Vanbrugh and Nash was a just and fitting tribute yet it is a great sadness to me that the father I lost in 1972 at the young age of ten should not have lived to see his father, the grandfather I never knew, restored to the popularity, admiration and greatness he justly deserved.

There is so much to be written about Lutyens that no one book – and there have been several – could hope to take it all on. This, to my certain knowedge, is the first volume to be devoted chiefly to Lutyens's interiors. The scope of my grandfather's devotion to detail was truly awe-inspiring. Throughout his career, Lutyens designed the furniture and fittings that went into his houses and public buildings. He was concerned as much with the look of the inside as that of the outside and the care he took with detail was second only to his remarkable ability to see a vision of a scheme as an utterly homogenous totality.

When you think that, in the creation of New Delhi, Lutyens was responsible for the city plan, several of its key buildings and monuments, and Viceroy's House itself. Yet in that 'house' – a building that dwarfs Versailles – he designed, in addition to virtually every single piece of furniture, not only the fireplaces but the ironmongery, not only the doors but the door knobs, not only the ceiling details but the chandeliers suspended from them. He even found time to attend to the clock, barely six inches high, disguised as a comic figurine, which stood on the nursery mantelpiece. Not all his buildings, or more to the point, all his clients offered such scope for fine detail but he was single-minded in terms of his design ethic and the Lutyens idiom is instantly recognisable in each small touch of a room.

Until recently, at least with respect to Lutyens's domestic architecture, this has not been particularly well known (or perhaps, more accurately, lacking in the attention it deserves), largely because when buildings changed hands the furniture tended to move with the previous incumbents. Indeed, over the course of the century, the interiors of many of his buildings have changed substantially. This fact of itself has made this book a tremendously difficult undertaking, and my respect and admiration go to all those who have worked so hard to put it together. I hope that the result will be an inspiration not only to those few lucky enough to own a Lutyens house but also to all those interested in bringing a unique and very creative stylistic approach into the decoration and furnishings of their own homes.

Lutyens was nothing if not single-minded in the creation of his buildings and thus it was in his interiors as well. Within those interiors, as a fundamental constituent part, were his wonderful and often unusual designs for furniture. We are fortunate in that many drawings and images of the furniture survive and I am proud that, in my own small way, I have contributed to the legacy of my grandfather (and also that of my father, who, himself, strove so hard to protect his memory) through my own recreation of Lutyens designs and interiors. Discovering, exploring, learning and building has been a labour of love that has occupied much of my life over the past decade. In doing so I like to think I have brought a little bit of Lutyens into many homes. I hope that this book will also bring enjoyment and a

ABOVE: *Lady Emily, in the early years of her marriage to Edwin Lutyens, with her elder children, Barbara (b. 1898), known as 'Barbie', and Robert (b.1901).*

slice of Lutyens into your home. It has been a pleasure being associated with its production and with it, I believe, another aspect of the legacy of one of our greatest architects will open the eyes of a new generation and his name will live on.

INTRODUCTION

For Edwin Lutyens, architecture was 'building with wit'. A designer of genius and a hugely successful one, during the course of a long career that began at the end of the nineteenth century and ended halfway through the twentieth, Lutyens was responsible for more than 550 buildings and projects, both in Britain and around the world. As Britain's unofficial 'architect laureate', his grand public commissions ranged from Viceroy's House in New Delhi and the British Embassy, Washington DC, to the Cenotaph in Whitehall. But his reputation was founded on the many private houses he designed around the turn of the century for prosperous, progressive clients; schemes on which he often collaborated with the great garden designer Gertrude Jekyll. It is in the domestic realm of these country houses and gardens that Lutyens's originality can most clearly be appreciated today.

From monuments to private houses, Lutyens's work displays a remarkable synthesis of function and artistry. Rooted in the constructional integrity of the Arts and Crafts movement but increasingly inspired by the pure logic of classicism, Lutyens's brilliance was to breathe new life into traditional forms and themes. Austere yet rich, grand yet domestic, houses such as Orchards, Grey Walls, Goddards, Castle Drogo, Munstead Wood and Deanery Garden are powerful expressions of what one might term a national aesthetic. It is Lutyens's reconciliation of extremes, the defining characteristic of his design approach, which marks this accomplishment as particularly English.

Equally typical is the sense of playfulness and delight that comes from absolute control. In an extraordinary career remarkable for its breadth of interest and achievement, the scope of Lutyens's work was all-encompassing: from the design of kitchen tables and nursery light fittings to the exquisite miniature of Queen Mary's Dolls' House; from war memorials to plans for the reconstruction of London after the Blitz. The notion of 'taste' – an instinctive sense of rightness in design – informed every creative decision, down to the choice of materials, colour schemes and the details of finishes and furniture. Like many great designers, his work consequently bears an identifi-

LEFT: *The hall at Heathcote, Ilkley, Yorkshire (1906). The columns are of green Siberian marble. The star lantern light fittings were a favourite of Lutyens.*

RIGHT: *Goddards, one of Lutyens's early Surrey houses, was commissioned by Frederick and Margaret Mirrielees as a holiday home for 'ladies of small means'.*

able stamp, a signature which is uniquely his own. Standing outside style and aesthetic movements, marrying the vernacular with the classical, the formal and the natural, the result is an important and enduring legacy of design.

This book focuses on the interior quality of Lutyens's great houses, from both a design perspective and from the point of view of style and expression. Lutyens took care to ensure that his houses would be supremely liveable; his ideas about light, colour, the interrelationships of indoor and outdoor spaces, demonstrate the humanism of his vision. His many designs for furniture and fittings to accompany these houses are a critical aspect of the integrity and unity he was able to achieve.

The sheer quantity and scope of Lutyens's design

output, and the great number of completed projects, mean that any book must be selective when presenting an account of his wide-ranging achievements. Chapter One, The Last Traditionalist, presents a necessarily abbreviated summary of his life and career, to provide a context in which his domestic designs can be appreciated. Chapter Two, Building with Wit, explores architectural themes arising from Lutyens's treatment of indoor and outdoor spaces, while Chapter Three, Taste, is an account of Lutyens's decided ideas on decoration and furnishing, many of which he expressed in his own homes. Throughout, the book features a selection of his more famous domestic designs, with some interior views photographed for the first time, revealing key elements and architectural details that evoke his original style. A selection of some of Lutyens's furniture designs, largely from the period in which he was involved in the planning and building of New Delhi, are currently produced by Lutyens Design Associates, a company set up by Candia Lutyens, Lutyens's granddaughter, and her husband Paul Peterson, with pieces made to order from the original drawings.

Every age has its opposing tensions. The countervailing directions of tradition and modernity have constituted the design argument of the twentieth century. In recent years, design has increasingly turned its back on tradition: tradition has been seen as a

Left: Little Thakeham, Sussex (1902) is a good example of a romantic or picturesque Lutyens design. Lutyens himself reckoned the house was 'the best of the bunch'.

dead end, a meaningless reiteration of historical styles, copied into a context where it is no longer relevant. For Lutyens, by contrast, tradition was living and vital. It was invention and adaptation as much as continuity, originality as much as cherished, time-honoured forms. It was, above all, free expression within a set of rules.

The opposition of tradition and progression is in many ways a false one. Both Frank Lloyd Wright and Le Corbusier, architects of more secure reputation, admired Lutyens's work, particularly for its dramatic spatial sequences. Frank Lloyd Wright kept the three *Memorial* volumes, published by *Country Life* after Lutyens's death, on his desk. It has been the twentieth century's loss that other architects and critics have not been able to see past the historical elements of Lutyens's approach to the underlying verities. As the architectural critic Roderick Gradidge has remarked, in Lutyens's work 'there was no attempt to be forward-looking, nor for that matter to be backward-looking. The buildings are built in the way that they are built because Lutyens thought that they would look best like that and that they would best suit his clients that way.'

Superficially, Lutyens can be seen as 'the last traditionalist', a designer whose vocabulary was both framed and enriched by precedent. Yet while he was certainly no modernist, his work does not represent a rejection of modern life, nor an ignorance of its requirements. His genius was to reinvent, rewrite traditions in such a way that they lived again. A master manipulator of space who was acutely sensitive to site and context, Lutyens played the 'high game' of architecture with consummate ease.

ONE

THE LAST TRADITIONALIST

To summarize a career as long and varied as Lutyens's, packed with people, places and events, inevitably requires the taking of certain liberties. It was a life full of detail; equally it was a life that has been well documented. Lutyens lived at a time when letter-writing had not yet been supplanted by more cursory forms of communication. His letters to his wife, from whom he was often away for long periods, amount to a personal journal, providing valuable insight into the thoughts and feelings that lay behind his architectural work. Like all his letters, they are also revealing of the curious quirks of his personality, quirks which would be irrelevent except for the fact that, as irrepressible flights of fancy and visual puns, they also crop up from time to time in his work in built form.

Given Lutyens's vast output, which encompassed alterations, renovations and improvements as well as new building, only selected schemes have been explored in depth to illustrate common threads and themes. Many of these great houses were built in the Edwardian era for clients of a similar background, more than a few of whom knew each other or shared intellectual, familial or social connections. For simplicity's sake, and to focus on the architecture, here such detail has been kept to a minimum. Similarly, as Lutyens became a public figure and moved in the highest levels of society, he encountered many of the most famous names of the century: politicians and painters, writers and heads of state. The architect who could tease the redoubtable Queen Mary was the same architect who demonstrated drawing techniques to Winston Churchill and dined with Augustus John.

This brief outline of his life is intended to provide both a flavour of one of the most intriguing personalities of the early twentieth century and a basic chronology of the development of his approach to design – a context in which to appreciate Lutyens's

RIGHT: *Tigbourne Court (1899), Surrey, viewed from the entrance court. The walls are made of local Bargate stone banded with red tile.*

unique style, particularly as expressed in the finest of his domestic buildings. Lutyens was a somewhat paradoxical figure: at once deadly serious and exuberantly playful. In the same way, his architecture synthesized apparently irreconcilable extremes: the austere logic of classical forms and the evolving vernacular of a native tradition.

EARLY LIFE

Edwin Landseer Lutyens was born on 29 March 1869, the eleventh of fourteen children born to Charles Henry Augustus Lutyens (1829–1915) and Mary Gallwey (1833–1906). He had nine elder brothers (two of whom, together with an unnamed stillborn baby, died in infancy) and one elder sister. Three more children followed Edwin.

The Lutyens family, originally of Dutch descent, comprised a number of prominent professional men, among them successful city merchants and army officers. Charles Lutyens, the son of General Charles Lutyens, shared both his family's military bent and fondness for the hunt. While stationed in Canada, as a captain in the Lancashire Fusiliers, Charles Lutyens was one of the founders of the Montreal Hunt; and it was here that he met his wife, Mary Gallwey, an Irish beauty who was the sister of Thomas Gallwey, the Governor of Montreal. Mary, a devout woman, had been born a Catholic but later converted to Evangelical Protestantism. Before the Crimean War, Charles was posted back to England; after the war was over he resigned his commission and applied himself to what up to now had been only a hobby: painting. The Lutyenses moved to London and in

1864 bought 16 Onslow Square, where Edwin was born; it was to be their London home for the next forty years.

Given his sporting enthusiasms, it is not surprising that Charles should choose to study under Sir Edwin Landseer, one of the most renowned of all painters of animals. Like Landseer, he chiefly earned his living painting horses and hounds, but other subjects included the Surrey landscape around the Lutyens' country home in the village of Thursley. The big rambling house, bought in 1876 at the peak of the artist's success, and misleadingly named The Cottage, was where Edwin and his brothers and sisters spent a large portion of their childhoods. Thursley was in the heart of what was then still a very rural area of trout streams and peaceful villages nestling amid farmland.

Edwin Lutyens was named after his father's friend and artistic mentor. His mother, however, is said to have refused Landseer's offer to adopt the child on the grounds that Landseer led a less than upright life. Ned, as Edwin preferred to be known throughout his life, adored his gentle, religiously minded mother from whom he inherited his dark hair and imaginative turn of mind. A serious childhood illness, thought to have been rheumatic fever, set him apart from his brothers and sisters. Unlike his more robust brothers, who were sent away to be educated at public school, Ned was considered too delicate to leave home. The result was that Ned's closeness to his mother deepened, while his intellectual development was free to follow its own course. Without this accident of upbringing, it is difficult to conceive how

Lutyens's great originality would have had the opportunity to flourish. As he later remarked to Osbert Sitwell: 'Any talent I may have was due to a long illness as a boy, which afforded me time to think, and to subsequent ill-health, because I was not allowed to play games, and so had to teach myself, for my enjoyment, to use my eyes instead of my feet. My brothers hadn't the same advantage.'

It is remarkable how often solitary and sickly childhoods provide the ideal circumstances for the emergence of distinctive artistic vision. Another great architect, Charles Rennie Mackintosh, who shared Lutyens's acute sympathy for nature and place, was similarly an invalid child, forced upon his own resources and largely educated without conventional restrictions. Ned, sporadically taught at home by his sisters' governesses and his brother Fred, who later became a painter, had plenty of time to roam around the countryside, hone his observational powers and feed his unfettered and inquisitive mind. From earliest days what fired his imagination and aroused his interest were the picturesque vernacular buildings of rural Surrey – farmhouses and manors, cottages and churches – traditional buildings made in the time-honoured way from timber, brick, wattle and daub, thatch, stone and tile and which seemed almost to grow out of the landscape.

This largely self-taught child invented his own way of seeing. Rather than sketch on paper, he used a small sheet of glass, drawing the view it framed using a sliver of sharpened soap. The method was undoubtedly inspired by a need for economy, but the result was a quick appreciation of perspective and how different planes of buildings related to each other and to a particular setting. A means of looking, rather than a means of recording, his glass pane, rinsed clear for every outing, served to develop his prodigious visual memory. Throughout his life, Lutyens frowned upon the common practice of keeping a sketchbook as a repository for ideas that could later be assimilated into buildings. Buildings, he believed, should emerge from their local context and not comprise disparate elements and design ideas borrowed from radically different locations.

But Lutyens's delight in the picturesque was not solely an aesthetic preference. The pragmatic side of his character, inherited from his father's family, expressed itself in a deep curiosity about how such buildings were made, along with a certain mathematical aptitude. Ned became a frequent visitor to building sites, carpenters' shops and builders' yards in the quest for knowledge about the variety of craft and construction techniques that had been employed for centuries to create such 'architecture without architects'. At this time, in the closing decades of the nineteenth century, there was still much traditional craft and lore to be learned; skills that would all but vanish over the next half century. In *Edwin Lutyens: A Memoir*, Mary Lutyens writes about her father: 'From old Tickner [the village carpenter] he learnt the ways of wood and how to recognise when the oak was ready for felling by the taste of the acorn.' Such arcane subtleties are hard to imagine today.

If Lutyens's unusual childhood gave him a vocation and allowed him to acquire invaluable tools for its subsequent pursuit, it also marked him emotionally.

Throughout his life he remained acutely aware of his academic shortcomings, suspicious of words, particularly well-turned phrases, and uneasy with male peers who had been more formally educated. His occasional gaucheness in polite company, fondness for pranks, puns and off-colour jokes – his propensity to act as 'the *enfant terrible* of the dinner table' in the words of his biographer Christopher Hussey – related to this fundamental shyness and sense of social inadequacy. It is possible that his manner may have cost him potential commissions; it is likely that it led people to underestimate the acuity of his mind. Lutyens's more or less constant punning, which struck many as puerile, seems more a symptom of mental agility. The mind that delighted in turning words inside out was simply the same mind that could conceive a design in three dimensions and review it from all angles and vantage points.

When his work became better known, the contrast between what he accomplished in building and his outward personality remained something of a puzzle for his admirers. Only with women, particularly older women, was Lutyens more comfortable, an ease which reflected his relationship with his mother. How central his mother was in his emotional landscape can be gauged by the fact that his wife-to-be was under the impression for some time that he was the only son of a widow.

One older woman, Barbara Webb, to whom he became deeply attached, was the first person to realize the true nature of his talents and to encourage them. Mrs Webb and her husband Robert, a typical country squire, lived not far away from Thursley, in the gracious surroundings of Milford House, a Georgian manor near Godalming. The house provided Lutyens with his first direct exposure both to the classical tradition in architecture and to a more refined style of life. Despite her conventional marriage, Barbara Webb was a highly intellectual and free-thinking woman with connections to London society and, through her brother, to India. Milford House became something of a refuge for Lutyens, an escape from the bohemian surroundings at home and the noisy turbulence of family life.

In 1885, when he was nearly sixteen, Lutyens went up to London to study architecture at the South Kensington School of Art (later the Royal College of Art). Given the single-mindedness of his childhood interests, there was an inevitability about his choice of study, matched by an equal determination on Lutyens's part to become 'successful'. Lutyens, with very little experience of formal education, did not stay the course at art school and remained there only two years. But, in common with many of his fellow students, he was a ready convert to the ideas of Ruskin, William Morris and Philip Webb. Webb, the architect of Morris's Red House, was a particular hero: the Arts and Crafts ideals of honest craftsmanship and simplicity must have spoken directly to a young man who had spent much of his life studying buildings where precisely those ideas were expressed.

Lutyens left college in 1887 to be apprenticed to Ernest George, a London architect with a busy practice. Apprenticeship, in those days before architectural degree courses, was the accepted means for would-

Right: Lutyens as a young man, photographed about the time when he was first setting up in practice.

be architects to acquire the necessary technical training. Lutyens's technical training was to last about six months.

While he was a pupil Lutyens met Herbert Baker, with whom he would later work on the design of New Delhi. Baker, public-school educated and an excellent sportsman, had many of the qualities which Lutyens felt he himself lacked; despite or perhaps because of this, the two became firm friends and went on walking and architectural tours together. Baker later remembered that Lutyens appeared to do very little work at the office and spent a good deal of time joking: 'He puzzled us at first, but we soon found that he seemed to know by intuition some great truths of our art which were not to be learned there,' he recalled in *Architecture and Personalities*. Equipped with his 'great truths', Lutyens soon found pupilage constraining. In 1888, when he secured his first commission, he left Ernest George to set up in practice on his own.

IN PRACTICE

Architecture is a long game: forty is young in a profession where many great practitioners reach middle age before building their first major scheme. Lutyens was barely twenty when he set up his own office in Gray's Inn Square. Even taking into account the unregulated nature of architectural training at the time, it was a considerably bold move and revealed the extent of his self-belief. But there was characteristic levelheadedness behind this dash for independence.

Lutyens's first commission was to build a nine-bedroom house at Crooksbury near Farnham, Surrey, for Arthur Chapman, a friend both of the Lutyens family and of Barbara Webb. Lutyens himself knew Chapman and his wife well, which represented a good start for interpreting a client's needs and wishes. Furthermore, he knew the countryside where the house was to be built like the back of his hand. A small legacy of £100 from Landseer's sister gave him the financial backing he needed and he engaged a rather elderly former builder to act as his assistant.

A further reason for Lutyens's decision to set up his own practice must have been the increasing financial difficulties in which his father was beginning to find himself. Horse and hound paintings were no longer as popular as they once had been and the family income had dwindled pitifully. Charles was going blind and already showing signs of the paranoia that would be a dominant feature of his old age: his eccentric response to hardship was to save money in odd ways – banning meat from the household, using newspaper for tablecloths and mending his own boots. Resigning his pupilage was one way Lutyens could ease the strains on his family, but it also represented a determination to become 'successful' financially and avoid suffering from the same circumstances himself. The growing untidiness and bohemian disarray at home offended his nature; his terror of poverty drove what would be a remarkable work rate throughout his career. Some notion of the efforts this entailed can be gleaned from the fact that, at Lutyens's death, over 80,000 drawings were recovered from his office; 70 per cent of these related to projects which failed to go ahead.

Lutyens began in practice as he meant to go on, socializing rarely and working late every night. As these early years went by, his confidence grew. While Crooksbury was being built, he had been so worried about the job and his abilities that he tended to visit the site after the workmen had gone home. The house, which Lutyens was subsequently engaged to extend twice, was derivative of the work of Norman Shaw, whom Lutyens greatly admired. But if it was not in the same league as the best of his architectural work it had one extremely important outcome. Through the Crooksbury commission, Lutyens met someone who was to become one of the key figures in his life and career: Gertrude Jekyll.

Gertrude Jekyll, one of the greatest of all garden designers, was twenty-five years older than Lutyens, a forthright and accomplished woman of diverse talents. Her first love, for painting, was set aside as her eyesight began to deteriorate, but she brought an artist's sensibility to planting, conceiving landscapes where swathes of colour accentuated complementary forms and shapes. She and Lutyens hit it off at once. Lutyens, who nicknamed everyone he was fond of – Barbara Webb was the 'Blessed Barbara' or 'Baa Lamb' –

ABOVE: *A sketch by Lutyens of Gertrude Jekyll (from a letter, c. 1896), whom he nicknamed 'Bumps' – 'the mother of all the bulbs' – in reference to her figure.*

RIGHT: Munstead Wood, *the house that Lutyens designed with Miss Jekyll, was an important early commission and won him critical recognition for the first time in his career.*

called Miss Jekyll 'Bumps', 'the mother of all the bulbs', in joking reference to her stout figure.

Gertrude Jekyll was living with her mother at Munstead House near Godalming when she met Lutyens, but had always dreamed of building her own house. Since 1883 she had been creating a garden on the proposed site for the house, in a wood across the road from the family home. Lutyens first designed and built a small cottage, The Hut, on the land. Then, in 1896, he began the design of Munstead Wood, Miss Jekyll's long-awaited house, and a commission which would win him the first important critical recognition of his career. An exceptionally sensitive interpretation of a client's desires and tastes, Munstead Wood was all the more remarkable for being created in the context of what was already a mature garden, responding to the planted design in layout and orientation with utmost sympathy.

Through Gertrude Jekyll, Lutyens met many of his subsequent clients, a glittering circle of wealthy but cultured people that included Queen Victoria's daughter, Princess Louise, later Duchess of Argyll, and, most importantly, Edward Hudson, who founded *Country Life* in 1897, an illustrated magazine which prominently featured much of Lutyens's work from 1900 onwards.

But it was Barbara Webb who made the next momentous introduction. Around the time he was beginning to design Munstead Wood, Lutyens met Lady Emily Lytton, at a musical soirée he attended in Mrs Webb's company. Emily Lytton was the daughter of Robert, the first Earl of Lytton, who had been the very first viceroy of India. Although the family could trace its ancestry back well over seven hundred years, the late earl had left very little money and the ancestral home, Knebworth, had had to be let. It was accepted by all concerned that Emily would have to marry well.

Lutyens fell in love with Emily virtually on sight. In the autumn of 1896, Barbara Webb invited Emily to stay in a tacit encouragement of the relationship. While Emily was at the Webbs', Lutyens introduced her to Miss Jekyll; the pair had suppers at The Hut, cycled about the countryside and talked about their plans for the future. On at least one occasion they cycled over to one of the neighbouring Surrey houses Lutyens had designed and forced their way into the unoccupied building by moonlight.

In the nine-month interlude that followed, the romance had something of the plot of a late Victorian novel. Emily, initially reluctant, was won over by Ned's torrent of affection poured out in letters, until her mother, Lady Lytton, stepped in and forbade further communication: an architect, even a promising one, was no catch for the daughter of an earl. All hopes seemed dashed when a timely intervention by Emily's sister convinced Lady Lytton to reconsider. Emily asked her uncle to review Lutyens's financial prospects and, again through the intermediary of Barbara Webb, a meeting was arranged where Lutyens, armed with several years of balance sheets, argued his case. The marriage was approved, on condition that Lutyens took out substantial life insurance, a not inconsiderable financial strain at this early stage in his career.

Lutyens's love letters to his wife-to-be, a breathless

RIGHT: The 'Casket' was a love token that Lutyens designed and had made for his future wife, Lady Emily. It contained various treasures with private meanings, including a crucifix designed by Lutyens, a heart and an anchor. In the bottom compartment was a tiny drawing of 'the little white house' the couple dreamed of building one day.

mixture of barely articulated passion and hope, illustrated with comic sketches and visual puns, leave no doubt about the seriousness of his intentions. But the most persuasive argument of his courtship, typically, came in built form. For Emily, Lutyens designed The Casket, an elaborately decorated miniature chest with drawers and secret compartments housing a number of charms and treasures with their own special, private meanings, together with a tiny drawing four inches square of 'the little white house' they both dreamed of building one day.

The details of their courtship and subsequent life together can be found in Mary Lutyens's memoir of her father, which is equally a poignant portrait of a marriage. Although a full account of this marriage lies outside the scope of this book, Lutyens's work cannot be properly understood without some appreciation of what was at times an unusual and unhappy relationship. In Emily, Lutyens was seeking both a romantic muse for his art and a bedrock for family life. Emily, both passionate and intellectual, with an underlying strain of melancholy in her character, could barely have conceived the supporting role she would have to play to her husband's prior commitment to architecture. It is probably true to say that they misread each other's personalities no less than their most intimate desires; in a reticent period where people simply lacked the language to remedy such misapprehensions, estrangement was the inevitable result.

On 4 August 1897, when Ned and Emily married at Knebworth, all this was in the future; the only sadness which marred this happy period in their lives was the death of Barbara Webb, who had been gravely ill for some time. Their first married home was 29 Bloomsbury Square, formerly the office of Norman Shaw. Much too large and much too expensive, the decision to take the house set a trend that kept money worries to the forefront for the rest of their lives. In this context, however, Lutyens's plans for their new home together, its furnishings and decoration, down to the last detail, provide a revealing indication of the emergence of his concept of 'taste'.

The new couple moved to Bloomsbury Square in the winter of 1897, Lutyens establishing his office on the ground floor, a separation of the professional and domestic under the same roof that would persist for over a decade. The following year their first child, Barbara, was born. New clients, a growing reputation, sympathetic publicity, a wife to support his endeavours and a baby daughter – it was all a young architect could conceivably want.

FROM PICTURESQUE TO WRENNAISSANCE

In the decade or so that followed, Lutyens established himself as one of the leading architects of the Edwardian period, a reputation almost entirely founded, at this stage, on designs for country houses. It was a period which also marked an aesthetic shift, from the early romanticism of Munstead Wood and nearby Orchards to the classicism of Nashdom and Heathcote. Yet, just as classicism never entirely supplanted Lutyens's more 'romantic' and poetic vision, evidence of classical inspiration can be seen quite early on in his career.

ABOVE: *Julia Chance in the garden at Orchards. The Chances commissioned Lutyens to design their new house at Godalming after seeing Munstead Wood in the final stages of its construction.*

Lutyens came to view classicism as just as integral to the national tradition as the vernacular farmhouses he so admired. It was Lutyens's particular genius to try to reconcile what at first sight seem opposing directions: the picturesque, with its use of local materials, response to site and charming irreg-

ularity; and the classical, with its rigorous logical demands deriving from the blueprint of the classical orders, and universality of application.

The first great houses Lutyens designed demonstrably fell within the picturesque or Arts and Crafts camps, from Orchards (1898) to Little Thakeham (1902). They share a similar vocabulary of asymmetric planning following the lay of the land, differing façades forming complementary compositions and the use of local materials traditionally worked. Orchards was a commission that came about

through a stroke of luck. The clients, Mr and Mrs Chance, already had a site at Godalming and an architect for their new house – Halsey Ricardo, who was an old friend – when they happened to spot Munstead Wood in the final stages of construction. Mrs Chance later remembered:

> Passing through a sandy lane we saw a house nearing completion, and on the top of a ladder a portly figure giving directions to some workmen. The house was a revelation of unimagined beauty and charm, we stood entranced and gazing, until the figure descended and we found ourselves, after due explanation, being welcomed as future neighbours.

Miss Jekyll, the 'portly figure' up the ladder, seized on this encounter to extol her young architect's brilliance. Somehow everyone's scruples were eventually overcome and Lutyens replaced Ricardo as the architect for the new house.

Described by Christopher Hussey as 'a symphony of local materials, conducted by an artist, for artists', Orchards was designed, like many of Lutyens's early houses, for people of substantial means but refined sensibilities, with their own views on what constituted beauty and good taste. By modern standards large, with four or five servants' bedrooms as well as

four or five master bedrooms, Orchards was nevertheless workable and liveable in an age of plentiful domestic labour. While the Chances were well off, as were all of Lutyens's clients, the establishment was far from grand, compared to the stately surroundings of a Knole, a Wilton or a Blenheim – the settings for many of the country house parties of the age. Indeed, the scale of Lutyens's houses was subsequently to put them increasingly at risk. Too large for the servantless households of the postwar era, but not big enough to immediately register as national treasures worth preserving, many have had somewhat chequered histories of use and occupancy.

If Lutyens's commissions in this busy period of his career were not always due to such fortuitous 'chance' encounters (he could not resist the pun), most came about by following up introductions and recommendations within a fairly close-knit sector of society. To keep in work, it was necessary for Lutyens to take every opportunity to move in such circles; his off-beat charm and jovial manner became a factor in persuading potential clients that he alone could design what they had always dreamed of building, swiftly sketching ideas or comic 'sketchiatures' on the pocket notepad he called a 'virgin'. 'Keeping people up to the mark' was his term for a process that was fundamentally about touting for business. Such contacts were not the only means of getting work.

PREVIOUS PAGES: *Orchards took three years to build and is constructed out of the local 'rubble' stone , set off with bandings of red tile. Lady Chance was a sculptress and had a studio in the house.*

RIGHT: *Les Bois des Moutiers, Varengeville, was designed for a banker and his wife, and was Lutyens's first private commission abroad. The narrow vertical windows have an almost modernist appearance.*

Edward Hudson, for whom Lutyens designed Deanery Garden in Sonning on Thames, and later remodelled and rebuilt the ruins of Lindisfarne Castle, provided Lutyens with the 'oxygen of publicity', regularly promoting the architect's work in his publication, *Country Life*.

Lutyens's first commission for a private house abroad came to him via his wife's family and following his commission to design the British Pavilion at the Paris International Exhibition, to be held in 1900. Elements of his design for Le Bois des Moutiers at Varengeville, for a banker and his wife, M. and Mme Guillaume Mallet, suggest that if Lutyens had continued in the same vein, he might now be viewed more as an early modernist rather than the last traditionalist. Instead, in the years to come, Lutyens was to reach further back, to Greece and Rome, for inspiration.

Classical elements had always been present to a greater or lesser degree in Lutyens's work, but soon after the turn of the century, they began to come to the fore. Marshcourt (1901) and Little Thakeham (1902), described by Christopher Hussey as 'classical in all but style', are evidence of this shift. From 1904 onwards, such classicism became ever more apparent in houses such as Nashdom (1905), Folly Farm (1905–6), Heathcote (1906), Temple Dinsley (1908), Great Maytham (1909) and The Salutation

(1911). It was a prolific time: on a single day in 1906 Lutyens won the contracts on four major new houses. Inigo Jones and Wren, rather than Webb and Norman Shaw, were now his principal architectural heroes; classicism was 'the high game', architecture at its most sublime. 'Wrennaissance' was Lutyens's irresistible coinage for this great tradition, a tradition no less English than Italian.

Lutyens, an architect who was later to be much imitated in countless and often meretritious suburban 'Lutyenesque' interpretations, did not simply adopt classicism as a stylistic overcoat any more than he had previously simply copied traditional picturesque forms of building. What sets him apart from copyists past or present was his intellectual determination to use the architectural language to say what he had to say. In this context, his own writings are particularly illuminating. Classicism was 'a game that never deceives, [that] dodges never disguise. It means hard thought all through – if it is laboured it fails.' The classical orders were a blueprint, but they could not be applied without deep understanding. 'You cannot play originality with the Orders. They have to be so well digested that there is nothing but essence left. When right they are curiously lovely – unalterable as plant forms ... The perfection of the Order is far nearer nature than anything produced on impulse or accident-wise.'

PREVIOUS PAGES: Lindisfarne Castle was the country home of Edward Hudson, the proprietor of Country Life, *a magazine that regularly promoted Lutyens's work.*

RIGHT: The Salutation, Kent, a house in the Queen Anne style, designed in 1911. From around 1904 onwards, such classical inspiration was ever more evident in Lutyens's work.

Then again, if any one element is adopted or altered, the entire composition must be worked through:

> That time-worn doric order – a lovely thing – I have the cheek to adopt. You can't copy it. To be right you have to take it and design it … It means hard labour, hard thinking, over every line in all three dimensions and in every joint; and no stone can be allowed to slide. If you tackle it in this way, the Order belongs to you, and every stroke, being mentally handled, must become endowed with such poetry and artistry as God has given you. You alter one feature (which you have to, always), then every other feature has to sympathise and undergo some care and invention. Therefore it is no mean (game), nor is it a game you can play lightheartedly.

Here it is perhaps worth mentioning that Lutyens's intuition that the classical orders are 'nearer nature' than most other design systems, that as a blueprint the orders are as 'unalterable as plant forms', has been given some credence by mathematical investigations. These demonstate that natural forms such as shells, galaxies, the distribution of petals on flowerheads and other common examples from the living world share the same proportional underpinnings as classical architectural relationships such as the golden section. In the light of such studies, classicism does indeed seem to enshrine certain fundamental, even universal design truths, and they were truths which particularly spoke to Lutyens's mathematical cast of mind. As he would later write, he was of the firm belief that without Isaac Newton, there would not have been Wren.

Lutyens was to prove triumphantly that the classical orders did indeed belong to him, but this new direction had important consequences. The first, as has been mentioned, was that he set off down a route which diverged from the course of twentieth-century design. The second was his belief that the architect's role in a modern age must be to think and design 'in advance of and distinctly beyond the conceptions of the architect's fellow men'. What was required from the architect was 'super-thought': this stance, of the architect as interpretative artist, became increasingly difficult to maintain over the succeeding decades, when functionalism and cost control threatened to reduce design to the resolution of technical problems.

A hint of coming difficulties came about in 1907 when Lutyens was one of eight architects selected out of ninety-nine in an open competition to produce designs for County Hall, the proposed headquarters of the newly formed London County Council. For nine months he laboured long and hard over his scheme, only to find that the project was awarded to a then-unknown, Ralph Knott, who had broken one of the competition's rules by adopting a plan that arranged rooms on both sides of main corridors. The rejection of Lutyens's design, grander in conception and scale (and inevitably in cost), and which would have created an important presence on this crucial river site, represents one of the many examples of architectural and planning shortsightedness in the history of the capital.

RIGHT: Lutyens in later life, seated at his desk at Mansfield Street. He spent much of the second half of his career working on the design of New Delhi.

In a happier vein, 1907 also saw the finalization of designs for the reconstruction and extension of Lambay Castle for Cecil Baring and his family. The principal building work was complete by 1912, but Lutyens continued to build and make improvements at Lambay right up to the early 1930s. Cecil Baring, of Barings Bank, had made a romantic marriage to an American divorcée; Lambay, a small derelict castle on a largely uninhabited island in the Irish Sea, spoke directly to Lutyens's profoundly romantic sense of site. Using the same local materials of the earlier construction, he extended the castle to provide a new kitchen wing and guest accommodation, but, as with all his extensions, avoided the common pitfall of duplicating the original style of the old fortified house. The dominating feature of the new building was sweeping pantiled roofs and, enclosing the whole castle complex, Lutyens built a circular rampart. Lambay proved to be one of Lutyens's favourite commissions and he always enjoyed visiting the island; the Barings and their children became close friends of the Lutyens family.

As the Edwardian era drew to a close and Lutyens approached his fortieth birthday, he had achieved a formidable body of work, almost exclusively in the realm of private houses. The increase in his practice – and the increase in his family (all five children, Barbara, Robert, Ursula, Elisabeth and Mary, were born between 1898 and 1908) – led to his moving his office in 1910 to 17 Queen Anne's Gate. The move was merely a physical transplantation: despite the fact that both his professional office and his domestic household had co-existed under the same roof for more than ten years, the segregation had always been more or less total between the two.

While Lutyens remained devoted to his wife and children, this segregation and its attendant long hours and long absences was beginning to take its toll on his private life. Lutyens and Lady Emily were both shy, and after initial, rather unsuccessful attempts to foster his professional life through social engagements, Emily found motherhood a convenient and absorbing preoccupation. Lutyens was often away – on site, with clients or at weekend parties 'working to get work' – and when he was not away he put in prodigiously long hours. Among the few family friends the couple met on a regular basis was the playwright J.M. Barrie, for whom Lutyens designed stage sets, including those for *Peter Pan*. The Darling children's nursery was modelled on the

Left: One of Lutyens's happiest associations was with the Barings family, for whom he extended Lambay Castle. The sitting room with its distempered walls and plain furnishings was simple in the extreme.

night-nursery at 29 Bloomsbury Square and, according to Mary Lutyens, her father 'invented Nana'.

Towards the end of this period, Emily began to find a new outlet for her considerable emotional and intellectual frustrations. Her sister, Constance, became active in the women's suffrage movement; Emily turned first to suffragism and then to Theosophy, the cult religion promoted by Mrs Annie Besant and to which she was introduced by Mme Mallet, Lutyens's client at Varengeville. Theosophy, which asserted the truth of all religions, initially drew Lutyens and his wife closer together; Emily, with an absorbing intellectual and spiritual interest, was clearly happier. Ultimately, however, this interest was to drive them apart. One of Theosophy's tenets was a belief that every 2,000 years a divine World Teacher would be reincarnated on Earth. A young boy from Madras, called Krishnamurti, had been identified as this supernatural being. As Emily was drawn deeper into Theosophy she became a devoted follower of Krishnamurti, virtually adopting him and his brother, Nitya, as part of the family.

As the first decade of the twentieth century drew to a close, commissions for private houses were beginning to dry up. New taxes, brought in by Lloyd George's 'people's budget' hit the moneyed classes hard; many of Lutyens's domestic commissions during the latter part of this period were for extensions and renovations, rather than new buildings. He was acutely aware of the need to find new types of work. What is generally characterized as the 'Indian summer' of Edwardian England was in fact a time of upheaval and change masquerading in the amber tints of nostalgia: momentous change was coming, but it would take the upheaval of a world war for it to be fully revealed and realized.

During this uneasy time, Lutyens had a few important commissions which extended his horizons beyond the realm of the private client and beyond England itself. The first came about in 1908 when he was asked to act as consulting architect on the design of Hampstead Garden Suburb, a planned development to the north of London orchestrated by the philanthropist Dame Henrietta Barnett. Like Bedford Park, the 'garden suburb' designed in part by Norman Shaw in 1876–7, this venture prefigured the objectives of modern town planning with its emphasis on 'mixed use' development. At Hampstead Garden Suburb it was envisaged that artisans would live alongside more prosperous middle-class householders and that housing, laid out sympathetically with generous gardens and wide-spaced avenues, would cluster around the community centres of churches and educational institutes. Lutyens's chief contribution was the design of the Suburb's two churches, St Jude's and the Free Church, as well as the other public buildings in the centre of the development; he also designed a number of houses in North Square and Eskine Hill (1910). At Hampstead Garden Suburb, Lutyens achieved harmony without dull uniformity, order without stifling regularity; unlike many planned developments, the Suburb had its own, living character which remains to this day.

At the same time, Lutyens's international reputation was growing. He was invited to design the British Pavilion at the International Exhibition to be held in Rome in 1911, later reconstructed as the British School in Rome. Visits to Italy around this time gave him the opportunity to experience the architectural wonders of the classical world at first hand, and he was astonished to find that 'There is so much here in little ways of things I thought I had invented!! no wonder people think I must have been in Italy.' As with his work on Hampstead Garden Suburb, Lutyens's commission to design the Pavilion entailed frustrating dealings with committees, tiresome meetings which he characteristically enlivened by making comic sketches of the pompous participants without their clothes.

In 1910, Lutyens ventured even further afield when he was asked to design the Johannesburg Art Gallery. This South African excursion was his first long trip abroad. It also provided the opportunity to renew his friendship with Herbert Baker, companion from his pupilage days, who had set up in practice there and had been engaged to design the government buildings in Pretoria. Baker helped Lutyens weather some of the antagonism of the local architectural community, who were understandably aggrieved that such a prestigious commission had gone to an outsider. During his stay, Lutyens acquired another job, to design the Rand Regiments' Memorial.

On the long sea journey to South Africa, Lutyens wasted little of his precious working time. He had

RIGHT: *Castle Drogo, which took nearly 20 years to build, is a granite castle situated on Dartmoor in Devon. The original design for a symmetric building was trimmed due to unacceptable rising costs.*

taken an assistant with him and they set up an office on board ship, where they produced designs for one of the largest of his domestic commissions, a job which had come in just prior to his departure. This was for Castle Drogo, a £50,000 scheme to build a granite castle on Dartmoor, Devon, for J.C. Drewe. It was to be nearly twenty years in the making.

NEW DELHI

In 1911, Britain was still an imperial power. At the Delhi Durbar to mark his coronation George V announced that India would have a new capital. The seat of government, formerly at Calcutta, would be moved to Delhi. The decision to build New Delhi was chiefly political and aroused equal controversy among both the European and Indian communities.

It was the President of the Royal Institute of British Architects, Reginald Blomfield, who recommended that Lutyens should serve on the three-man commission to advise on the site and layout of the new city. Lutyens agreed on the condition that he would be allowed to design the principal government buildings. Although another architect, H.V. Lanchester, appeared to be in the running, Lutyens was invited to meet the King prior to his departure and was encouraged by his favourable reception. He set sail in April 1912.

The Delhi commission plunged Lutyens into the world of committees with a vengeance. His happiest working relationships had always been with sympathetic individual clients whom he could charm and cajole: clients who often ended up with houses quite different from what they had expected, costing quite considerably more, but who almost always grew to love the results. With private clients, architectural 'super-thought' could go more or less unimpeded. Dealing with colonial administrators, bureaucrats, viceroys and the panoply of the British imperial state was a vastly different matter. From the outset, Lutyens found himself embroiled in a complex web of political, economic and imperial convolutions. His notional client, the Viceroy, Lord Hardinge, was a skilled political operator, but proved not an easy man to pin down or win over.

Delhi represented precisely what Lutyens had long been hoping to secure: a project of monumental proportions that would give him the opportunity to set his seal on posterity. Little did he know that it would occupy much of the next eighteen years, almost the rest of his productive life; that it would bring immense frustrations and disappointments as well as acclaim; or that his grand design, carefully envisaged to last three hundred years, would have a direct political relevance for less than two decades. In a trite sense, Delhi proved a perfect example of the old warning: be careful what you wish for, for it might come true.

On his first visit, before he had been formally commissioned, his task as part of the expert party was to recommend a suitable site for the new city. The requirements were for an area of about 25 square miles which would not prove too costly to acquire or too distant from the existing city, and which would be fertile, irrigated and healthy, with room for future expansion. Another consideration was to avoid building over any of the many sacred sites and tombs which were scattered around the entire Delhi area. After weighing many alternatives, the commission finally recommended a flat area of fertile river plain south of old Delhi, between Indrapat in the east and the Ridge, an area of high ground to the west.

Towards the end of this first visit, Lutyens met Lord Hardinge and was pleased to find that the Viceroy seemed to agree with his rough proposals regarding the layout of the new city. He found Lady Hardinge even more sympathetic and began to form an idea of the various requirements that Government House would have to fulfil. Lutyens's initial estimate for the cost of this building was £1 million, five times more than what the Viceroy had expected. In plan, the development was to consist of a tree-lined processional avenue two miles long from Indrapat in the east to Government House in the west. Immediately in front of Government House would be a forecourt, leading to a Great Court flanked by two Secretariat buildings for the Civil Service.

While Lutyens returned to England to work up his designs in greater detail, Lord Hardinge inspected the proposed site and found it lacking. What he proposed instead was an elevated site on Raisina Hill in a commanding position overlooking Delhi, an area to the north-west of the site the commission had recommended. There was not enough ground area on top of the hill, but engineers had advised that the top could be levelled to make a flat site. Hardinge also wrote to Lutyens that he hoped the buildings would have 'an Indian motif', 'an oriental adaptation'. Even more alarmingly, he was considering putting the design of the Secretariat buildings out to competition and had asked Lanchester to draw up the rules.

Lutyens, despite having secured the King's approval for his sketch proposals after a visit to Balmoral, became increasingly uneasy. His response to this feeling of vulnerability was to look for an ally and he wrote to Herbert Baker to ask if he would be prepared to collaborate on the scheme. After some prevarication, Baker eventually agreed to meet Lutyens in India during his next visit in the winter of 1912–13.

Lutyens's second visit to India, the first of many subsequent winters he would spend there, was dominated by his struggle to convince the Viceroy that the design for the new buildings should not have an 'Indian' theme. As the following extract from a letter written at this time reveals, Lutyens's rejection of superficial Indian ornamentation did not mean he intended a wholly Western design: what he was attempting was a synthesis of East and West on the deepest aesthetic level:

> Though Lord Hardinge has great taste and is certainly what one would call artistic, I do no think he realises the use of ornament in relation to construction, where it should begin and end, and what is integral and what applied. He begins with ornament instead of construction …
>
> To express modern India in stone, to represent her amazing sense of the supernatural, with its compliment of profound fatalism and enduring patience, is no easy task.

This cannot be done by the almost sterile stability of the English classical style; nor can it be done by capturing Indian details and inserting their features, like hanging pictures on a wall!

In giving India some new sense of architectural construction, adapted to her crafts, lies the great chance of creating what may become a new and inspiring period in the history of her art …

It must be said that Lutyens's impressions of India do not always make sympathetic reading. He shared many of the prejudices of his age and class, prejudices no less unpalatable at times for their context. While he found India as a whole 'thrilling yet baffling' and grew to have great respect for Indian craftsmen, he was dismissive of both Hindu and Mogul styles of architecture, repelled by the disorder and cultural clamour of the cities and fundamentally unmoved by the mysticism which so intrigued his wife. Such opinions were by no means unusual, but they do make Lutyens's architectural achievements in India all the more surprising.

The opportunity to engage Lord Hardinge in this aesthetic debate was severely delayed when a home-made bomb was thrown at the Viceroy's elephant during his state entry into New Delhi just before Christmas 1912. Although his wife was unhurt, Lord Hardinge was seriously injured and took a long time to recover. It was not until February 1913 that Lutyens was officially appointed co-architect of New Delhi along with Herbert Baker, who had come out to join him.

Lutyens, who had never entertained the slightest notion of taking a partner in his architectural practice, now had a collaborator in the largest and most ambitious scheme of his career. During the long months of indecision and prevarication, he had sensed the need for an ally; in the event, that ally was to prove a thorn in the flesh. It had been understood and agreed from the outset that Baker would design the Secretariat buildings and Lutyens, Government House. When Baker arrived in India, he immediately proposed that the Secretariat buildings should be raised up to share the same elevated position as Government House on top of the new site at Raisina Hill: the idea was to create an 'acropolis'. This would entail moving Government House 400 feet back from the brow of the hill. Against his better judgement, Lutyens agreed to the proposal; its consequences would cause him bitter regret.

'Bedlampore' was Lutyens's exasperated coinage for New Delhi. It was a long, complex and exhausting scheme, made worse by intensifying differences between Lutyens and his collaborator. Baker, he was chagrined to find, was not entirely willing to fight the cause of architecture against the bureaucrats of the committees. Lutyens would spend nearly every winter in India until the new capital was officially opened in 1931, returning to England, and other commissions, in the summer months – a gruelling routine. He set up a separate office in Apple Tree Yard for the Indian work, but high Western expenses and low Eastern building costs meant that he earned very little money from all his efforts: his fees, in the standard way, were calculated on a percentage of the building costs.

ABOVE: An aerial view of New Delhi, showing Viceroy's House (formerly Government House) in the background, flanked by the two Secretariats in the foreground, designed by Baker.

An early headache came when Lord Hardinge cut the budget for Government House by half, entailing much redesign. A more devastating blow came in 1915 when Lutyens fully realized the consequence of moving the Secretariats up to the Raisina summit. The gradient of the slope up to the 'acropolis' – which he had himself approved on the basis that it was an interim proposal – now meant that most of Government House could not be seen for a significant proportion of the two-mile processional route. It was the Secretariats which now dominated the approach, with the top of the dome of Government House rather comically popping up between them. Lutyens had always intended that Government House, as the focus of the symmetrical layout, should remain at all times visible. He was utterly crushed by his discovery and frustrated when his attempts to remedy the situation were blocked. Relations with Baker descended to a new low, from which they barely recovered. Although there are several theories, no full explanation can be given as to why Lutyens, with his characteristic attention to detail, had not spotted this problem earlier.

Critics have not entirely shared Lutyens's disappointment; many, like Baker, have felt that the disappearance and re-emergence of Government House as it is approached along King's Way, the processional route, adds to the power and mystery of the design. What is undisputed is the remarkable synthesis of East and West that Lutyens managed to achieve in the design of Government House (named Viceroy's House in 1929).

Lutyens, who believed that classicism had universal relevance, had no qualms about designing the government buildings for New Delhi according to strict classical rules. Classicism, as an approach, is autocratic rather than assimilative: the underlying premise is that the rules work whatever the situation. But, as Lutyens demonstrated in all his classical designs, this did not mean simply applying the rules without adaptation. In the design of Viceroy's House he showed that he understood local conditions very well. Always sensitive to place, he extracted certain practical elements of Indian architectural styles, both Hindu and Mogul, and adapted them to the logic of the orders. In essence, he created an Indian version of how classicism could have developed in the subcontinent, and he achieved this, not by superficial decorative quotations, but through a deep understanding of the particular conditions imposed by both site and context.

In an early letter to Lord Hardinge he had sig-

LEFT: *The East Front of Viceroy's House, showing the blade-like cornice Lutyens adapted from Mogul design.*

nalled his intentions: his designs would show 'how natural and Indian a Western motif can look, treated for the Indian sun *with* Indian methods applied *without* throwing away the English tradition …' A central battle was to win Hardinge away from his insistence on the more oriental-looking pointed arch. Lutyens was insistent on the rounded arch, whose universality he defended vigorously in a letter to Baker: 'I should like to ask him [Hardinge] to what country the Rainbow belongs! One cannot tinker with a round arch. God did not make the Eastern rainbow pointed to show his wide sympathies.'

In bright light, form is dissolved. The shimmering mirage of the Taj Mahal seemed to Lutyens to lack substance as architecture. He believed, by contrast, that where the sun is strong, shadow is needed to delineate structure and reinforce the impression of solidity. Two typically Mogul features – the exaggerated blade-like cornice and the roof pavilion – were adopted by Lutyens in the design of Viceroy's House to provide such defining shadow. Solidity is also reinforced by the relatively small number and size of window openings. Heat is the enemy in a climate of extremes: much of the massive square footage of Viceroy's House – at 200,000 square feet, it is slightly larger than Versailles – is devoted to internal/external elements, open courtyards and loggias. Long, low horizontal lines typical of traditional Indian building reduce the impact of the height: 'a palatial development of the bungalow' is Christopher Hussey's appraisal. With its powerful presence and imperial dome, Viceroy's House has an inescapable political meaning. Yet, although it is demonstrably a classical building, it could not be anywhere else but India. In terms of architectural thought, Viceroy's House ultimately demonstrates that Lutyens understood India very well.

ARCHITECT LAUREATE

The tortuous work on New Delhi, which involved recasting the design many times according to changes in proposed accommodation, vacillations of budget and other complex factors inevitable when the client is effectively the State, went on in parallel with Lutyens's other commissions. The mounting workload, with its many distractions, was accompanied by increasing tensions at home. In 1914, while Lutyens was in India, the lease on Bloomsbury Square had expired and Emily had taken the lease on a new house, 31 Bedford Square. Lutyens never liked the new house, which was one he had previously considered and rejected before they were married. When war was declared in August, many of his staff volunteered, increasing the pressures of work; soon after, Emily, already vegetarian in accordance with her Theosophist beliefs, broke the news that she would henceforth be celibate.

War did not immediately halt progress on New Delhi and in the meantime Lutyens won the commission to design a palace in Spain, near Toledo, for the Duke of Peñaranda. The commission was particularly welcome since Lutyens was again worried about money. In happier times Mrs Besant had asked him to design a headquarters for the Theosophical Society in Tavistock Square; an ugly row had broken out over the progress of the building work which led to Lutyens's resignation. Yet another Theosophically connected upset occurred in 1916 when Emily publicly supported the political movement for Home Rule in India, a deep embarrassment for the architect of an imperial city. Mrs Besant prevailed upon Emily to desist from political activities but not before Emily had been roundly rebuked in print by Edward Hudson for neglecting her husband's interests.

In 1917 work was suspended on New Delhi for the duration of the war. In July, after Lutyens returned from India, he was asked to go to France, along with Baker and Charles Aitken, the Director of the Tate Gallery, to inspect the temporary war graves and report on the type of monuments that should be built to commemorate them. This sad duty was to have an important consequence: it led directly to the Cenotaph, a monument which brought Lutyens widespread public acclaim for the first time.

Immensely moved by the 'ribbons of little crosses' and the poignancy of the poppies and wild flowers growing over the graves, Lutyens's instinctive feeling was that the cemetery monuments should be in the form of 'great stones', eternal in spirit and non-denominational in character, and that the headstones for the graves should be of uniform design. Baker was in favour of the Christian symbolism of the cross. Their differing approaches – Lutyens powerfully abstract, Baker almost literal-minded – encapsulated the difficulties they had experienced working together on Delhi. In the event, a compromise was worked out: most of the cemeteries were marked by Lutyens's great stones of remembrance,

but other single-faith cemeteries had monuments incorporating religious symbols.

The last year of the war was a time of despondency for Lutyens. Work was not progressing, either at home or abroad, money was short and the family was dispersed. Emily was busy with her Theosophical activities and the younger children had been evacuated to the country when the zeppelin raids on London had increased in severity. In 1918 the lease ran out on Bedford Square; while not precisely homeless, the family lacked a permanent base.

In 1916 Lutyens had met Lady Sackville, mistress of Knole and mother of Vita Sackville-West. Lady Sackville, seven years his senior, was still a captivating woman and Lutyens was drawn to her warmth and frivolity. Their relationship, which lasted for the next decade, was tolerated, almost encouraged by Emily. Lady Sackville had a firm belief in Lutyens's genius and a passion for acquiring houses and altering them. Lutyens carried out many designs for her, and was paid as often in gifts as in money – the only car he ever owned, a Rolls-Royce, was a present from 'MacSack'. (In the context of their relationship, Lutyens himself was 'MacNed').

In July 1919, the Prime Minister, Lloyd George, sent for Lutyens to ask him to design a 'catafalque' in honour of the fallen, for the march past of allied troops planned in ten days' time. The march past, the first official act of remembrance after the Armistice, was to take place in Whitehall in the presence of Marshal Foch and General Pershing. Given the short notice, the monument would be a temporary structure, built of wood and plaster. Lutyens's immediate response was that 'catafalque', which means a coffin, was the wrong term; what was required was a 'cenotaph' or an empty tomb. It was not a word that had been in common usage before.

It took Lutyens about six hours to conceive the idea for the monument, which represents one of the most powerful distillations of classicism he had so far attempted. Eternal in spirit like his 'stones of remembrance' and with the air of inevitability of all great designs, the Cenotaph immediately caught the public mood. Within a week it was being talked about as a great national monument and letters of tribute for its designer poured in. Providing a solemn focus for the depth of national feeling aroused by one of the most traumatic of conflicts, its importance at this juncture of history for a country still trying to come to terms with the loss of so many of its young men can barely be appreciated today.

The apparent simplicity of the Cenotaph is based on an exquisite refinement of classical principles. As is the case in the Parthenon, there are no straight lines. Each horizontal or vertical is subtly inclined to provide visual correction – the 'entasis' of classicism. The verticals of the Cenotaph, if projected upwards, would meet at a point 1,000 feet above ground; the horizontals are sections of a circle's circumference with a theoretical centre point 900 feet underground. The mathematical calculations required for the finished design filled an entire exercise book. Lutyens, who had not been invited to the march past, was commissioned to rebuild the Cenotaph in a permanent form on the same site for Armistice Day 1920. He was subsequently to design ninety

other war memorials and cemeteries, including the Memorial to the 73,357 Missing of the Somme, at Thiepval, whose interlocking arches create eloquent voids that convey, more powerfully than any words, the devastation of missing lives.

He was Sir Edwin Lutyens by now, knighted in the New Year's Honours of 1918. In 1921 he was awarded the Gold Medal of the Royal Institute of British Architects, the highest honour in his profession; the Institute of American Architects followed suit in 1924. The Cenotaph had made him the best-known architect in the country; with the work on Delhi resuming at the beginning of the 1920s and commissions again building up after the lull of the war years, he was increasingly busy.

The Lutyenses once again had a home. In 1919, Lutyens bought 13 Mansfield Street with the aid of a loan from Lady Sackville. The house where he would live for the rest of his life was a larger version of Bloomsbury Square and he spent much effort having it decorated to his specification. It was in the dining room at Mansfield Street that one of the most charming of all Lutyens's designs was assembled: Queen Mary's Dolls' House.

The idea for this 'colossal trifle', as Christopher Hussey has described it, is said to have arisen at a dinner party attended by Princess Mary Louise and Lutyens, among others. The government was planning to hold a British Empire Exhibition in 1924 to mark the industrial recovery of the nation. Somehow the suggestion arose to create a model, at a scale of one inch to one foot, to serve as a record of a fine house of the period. It was just the sort of idea to

RIGHT: Lutyens walking away from the temporary Cenotaph, after the dedication ceremony in July 1919 (he was not invited). The memorial, which was completed in 1920, made him the best-known architect in the country.

ABOVE: *Dining room at Mansfield Street, Lutyens's final home, showing the original dining table Lutyens designed before his marriage.*

appeal to Lutyens's sense of fun. The Dolls' House was three years in the making and involved the labours of 1,500 people. Gertrude Jekyll worked on the garden, the artist William Nicholson contributed the murals and Lutyens himself drew up the design and insisted that, as far as possible, every fixture

should work. The Dolls' House, now on permanent display at Windsor Castle, has been extensively documented: there is even a book which catalogues the 350 tiny leather-bound works in the library. Queen Mary, who regularly inspected its progress, was delighted by it; this beautiful, intricately wrought miniature set the seal on Lutyens's status as architect laureate.

Throughout the 1920s, Lutyens continued to spend a large proportion of each year in Delhi, where work was progressing on Viceroy's House, and maintained his custom of keeping a shipboard office on the long journeys there and back. Quite a different political climate now existed in India. Constitutional reforms brought in by the British government at the end of the war had not allayed the rising tide of nationalism and the whole scheme for the imperial city was more controversial than ever. Quite apart from such political issues, building New Delhi was a massive endeavour. The size of the task can be gauged from the fact that 700 million bricks were used to build the carcass of Viceroy's House alone; the stoneyard supplying the dressed stone to clad the immense building was the largest of its kind in the world.

At home, it was an equally prolific time for the practice, with a total output for the decade, including war memorials, of some 180 works. Working with a small number of assistants and half a dozen draughtsmen in the main office at Queen Anne's Gate, Lutyens was involved in every aspect of every design, conceiving ideas, making constant revisions and checking every drawing thoroughly before issue.

RIGHT: *Queen Mary's Dolls' House in the front drawing room at Mansfield Street, where its contents were assembled over a period of two years. Queen Mary visited it here several times; her favourite item was the miniature stamp album donated by Stanley Gibbons.*

An inveterate pipe-smoker throughout his life, every day six little filled pipes were lined up along the side of his drawing board, ready for his constant ruminative play with pipe and matches.

In Lutyens's view, an architectural drawing was 'merely a letter to a builder telling him precisely what is required of him, not a picture wherewith to charm an idiotic client'. One of his assistants, W.A.S. Lloyd, later recalled Lutyens's working methods: 'He thought continually in three dimensions, if not four, and set no store by a drawing other than as a

BELOW: Lutyens at Mansfield Street in the 1920s, sitting in his favourite chair, the Napoleon chair, and characteristically smoking a pipe.

statement of intention. "Don't portmanteau it" was standard criticism of an over-crowded elaborate drawing.' At the same time, proportions, ratios, details, all had to be right and thought through to their logical conclusions; 'almost' or 'good enough' would never do. Achieving such standards added to the pace and pressure of a busy practice, with the inevitable consequence of regular 'panics' requiring all-night sessions to get drawings issued on time.

Although few commissions for large country houses came in after the war, Lutyens was often called back to remodel, extend and alter houses he had previously built. During this period, his work displays an even greater dedication to classicism, an original yet coherent mastery of the orders. In this vein, two commercial buildings in London are particularly notable: Britannic House (1920), designed as the headquarters of the Anglo-Iranian Oil Company, and Midland Bank, Poultry (1924.) The vigour and subtlety of these designs displays the architect's mature grasp of classical principles and his ability to manipulate the elements in such a way that the whole tradition was revitalized. Another Lutyens bank, Midland's Piccadilly branch (1922), designed in association with the bank's architects, forms an exquisite complement to Wren's St James's Church, beside it. In this context, the news that Lutyens's old partner and rival, Herbert Baker, had won the commission to rebuild the upper portion of the Bank of England above the colonnade designed by Soane, must have come as a bitter blow.

In 1920 Lutyens had been commissioned to reconstruct Gledstone Hall, a Georgian mansion bought by Sir Amos Nelson, a wealthy mill owner. He was to work in collaboration with a local architect, Richard Jaques. The collaboration went well, but the estimates for reconstruction came in too high and the client commissioned instead a new house to be built on a site in the Yorkshire moors. Gledstone Hall (1923) is a perfect example of Lutyens in his late classical mode. Subtle orchestration of façades and views are matched by the austere nobility of the interior, with its black and white scheme. A year later, at Tyringham Park, Buckinghamshire, Lutyens designed a classical landscape to complement the eighteenth-century house designed by Soane, a landscape which featured two temples, one a bathing pavilion and the other dedicated to music. The British Embassy, Washington DC, a Wrennaissance design with steeply pitched roofs, built on a difficult, sloping and restricted site, followed on in 1926.

The end of the decade saw Viceroy's House nearing completion. It was scheduled to be handed over in 1929, but the building had only been finally covered in 1928. Finishing the interior, with its specially designed fittings, furniture and furnishings, called for heroic efforts. Several viceroys had come and gone since the scheme was first proposed. Lutyens found Lord Irwin, Viceroy when he was working on the design of the interiors at the end of the 1920s, much more sympathetic than most. The House was handed over in 1929; Lutyens was back in India in January 1931 for the official opening of the new capital.

By this time, Lutyens had conceived the design for what would be the most complete summary of his architectural beliefs: Liverpool Cathedral.

Commissioned to design a new Roman Catholic cathedral by the Archbishop of Liverpool, Dr Downey, in 1929, Lutyens spent the following year working on the preliminary design, which was to be executed in grey granite. Superficially, it may seem unusual that an avowed agnostic, who detested the narrowness and bigotry that so often accompanied religious adherence, should find such a commission the fulfilment of a life's ambition. Lutyens, however, while refusing to subscribe to a particular set of beliefs, nevertheless had a deep religious sense; as he once wrote to a friend, 'au fond I am horribly religious, but cannot speak of it and this saves my work'. That spirituality, of which he was unable to speak, infuses the design of Liverpool Cathedral.

Increasingly convinced that artistic beauty could be proved to rest on deep underlying mathematical relationships and principles, Lutyens's design was an inspirational essay in pure geometric form. With its great dome rising out of solid cubed masses, the cathedral was nothing less than a three-dimensional squaring of a circle. The foundation stone was laid in 1933 and by 1940 enough of the design had been built for certain areas of the cathedral to be used as air raid shelters. But this grand design, a triumphant vindication of the enduring relevance of classicism in a modern age, was never to be completed. In 1959, with only the crypt complete, the work was stopped through lack of funds.

Lutyens's other religious work of this period was Campion Hall in Oxford, for the Society of Jesus. Built of local rubble stone, the building is austere and beautifully simple.

RIGHT: Interior of the Midland Bank, Poultry, designed by Lutyens in 1924, one of the architect's few large commercial schemes. Like many of his later designs, the Midland Bank displays a vigorous and confident handling of classical elements.

LAST YEARS

As with all architects, and indeed anyone involved in the construction industry in any capacity, Lutyens's fluctuating fortunes served as a barometer of changing economic, political and social conditions. Lutyens continued to receive honours, and the publication of the finished Viceroy's House brought fresh acclaim. But by the 1930s, when his separate office for handling the Delhi work was closed and his practice was brought together at new premises in Eaton Gate, the worldwide economic slump was proving a harsh climate in which to gain new commissions. The new income tax exacerbated his ever-present worry about money. El Guadalperal, the palace in Spain on which he had been working for many years, was a casualty of the Spanish Civil War. The Cathedral was his principal concern; other substantial work was harder to come by.

If professional life was more difficult, private tensions were easing. The purchase of Mansfield Street, when his older children were flying the nest, came too late to function as a real family home. But by the beginning of the 1930s, Emily had finally grown disenchanted with Theosophy and the spiritual life; the reunion with his wife provided Lutyens with emotional tranquillity in his later years. In 1932 he embarked on a tour of Greek and Near Eastern classical sites with his beloved daughter Ursula, one of the very few holidays he ever took. Four years later, when his son Robert, by now a successful architect in his own right, came to join him at Eaton Gate, a long and bitter rift between father and son – originally provoked by Robert's elopement at the age of nineteen – was finally mended.

In 1938, as war clouds loomed once more on the horizon, Lutyens embarked on what would be his final passage to India. He was going back to Delhi to repair and restore the decorations and garden of Viceroy's House to their original conception: a subsequent vicereine, Lady Willingdon, had made many unsympathetic alterations. (She was the sort of person who would put a bay window in the Parthenon if she owned it, he wrote.) Almost immediately Lutyens succumbed to a serious bout of pneumonia which nearly proved fatal. Upon his return, after a seemingly full recovery and the renewal of many old friendships, he learned that he had been made President of the Royal Academy. He was nearly seventy.

Since the mid-1930s Lutyens had been working as a consultant to Sir Charles Bressey on the preparation of a Highway Development Survey; the intention was to plan road infrastructure to accommodate London's future needs. The results of the survey were published in 1938. In 1940, Lutyens set up the Royal Academy Planning Committee to consider how best to reconstruct London after the widespread damage and devastation that was widely expected to follow from aerial bombardment, an expectation substantiated by the Blitz which began the following autumn. The Royal Academy Plan for London, 1942, based to some extent on the earlier Highway Survey, pleaded the architectural case in terms of urban planning. Many of its recommendations have since become standard practice. Other ideas – restoring Covent Garden, reconnecting the city with its river and enlarging the area around St Paul's – were dis-

RIGHT: Lutyens working in the racquet court, the top floor of the converted stables and coach house at Mansfield Street. The plans for Liverpool Cathedral can be seen in the background: 'the very greatest building that was never built', according to his son, Robert.

tinctly ahead of their time. Like Wren before him, Lutyens envisaged the use of symmetry and vista to bring a sense of grandeur and monumentality to a city which had developed organically and haphazardly.

In 1940 Lutyens had another severe attack of pneumonia, this time complicated by a thrombosis. Recovery was slow and by the end of 1941 he was increasingly troubled by a cough. The eventual diagnosis, of which he was not told, was cancer. He had little more than two years to live. Throughout this time, until he grew too weak, he continued to work on the Cathedral drawings, preparing for the time when the war would end and work would resume again on his greatest design.

By Christmas 1943, Lutyens was bed-ridden. He asked for some of the Cathedral designs to be brought to his bedroom and arranged where he could see them. Emily, who had nursed him devotedly, was ill herself with flu; his children and grandchildren gathered at Mansfield Street for the sombre holiday.

Lutyens died peacefully on New Year's Day 1944. The funeral was held in Westminster Abbey on 6 January. His ashes lie in the crypt of St Paul's Cathedral.

TWO

BUILDING WITH WIT

Lutyens was, first and foremost, a designer of houses. His early reputation was almost entirely based on work he carried out for private clients, and he continued to design houses right the way through his long career, while he was also designing churches and memorials, government buildings, commercial premises and banks. Even Viceroy's House, the seat of imperial power in India, comprises, in the Viceroy's residence, a signficant domestic element. Admittedly, many Lutyens houses were grand in scale: both palaces and castles were among his vast output. Yet, while few of these houses were modest by today's standards, no matter how grandly conceived the architectural effects, they always retained a humanist quality; they were imbued with life and vitality. As Christopher Hussey perceptively writes: '[Lutyens] had his amazing capacity to project his imagination into every space of whatever he was building, so that he lived the life of the people who would ultimately inhabit it, more vividly perhaps than they ever would themselves, and in a sense *became* the building.'

On first appraisal, the themes which Lutyens expressed in his houses might seem to have little relevance today. Even in a more commodious age he was profligate with space: the typical generosity of his stairs, landings, hallways and corridors has often been cited as evidence of an imbalance in his architectural planning. He was also designing at a time when there was plentiful domestic help to keep large households running smoothly. Only the seriously rich could afford to live in such an expensive style today, or to maintain an original Lutyens house in an appropriate fashion.

Nevertheless, there are good reasons for re-examining what Lutyens achieved in the design of these great houses. One of the most important concerns was the quality of space. In contemporary design, we have become obsessed with space in terms of simple size. There is almost a notion that the greater the

RIGHT: A staircase at Marshcourt is beautifully detailed in oak, with pegged joints and the stairs themselves fashioned from single pieces of timber.

amount of square feet we have at our disposal, the better our homes will necessarily be. Here Lutyens, the master manipulator of space, can be very instructive. He understood the great conundrum of space, the fact that quality derives from experience, contrast and theatre, and is not the inevitable result of how much area a room encloses. Lutyens excelled at making houses seem bigger than they actually were, both from within and from without.

Lutyens houses are houses that provoke an immediate response, houses where one immediately wants to live. In essence, the Lutyenesque house is an ideal house: its qualities enshrine dreams of living. This is not surprising, since Lutyens himself was drawing on earlier examples – Georgian country estates, Elizabethan manors, moated castles – and distilling their romance in his own turn-of-the-century designs. What gives his houses a special poignancy is this Edwardian context, a period on the cusp of the modern age, when traditions were cherished all the more for being on the brink of disappearance. It is a poignancy which is expressed in the literature of the time: in *A Room with a View* and *Howard's End*, as much as *The Wind in the Willows*, and the children's stories by E. Nesbit, houses and places have as much character and presence as people. Edwardian attitudes to living, at once progressive and traditional, settled and informal, still underpin our concepts of what a home should be. On the other side of two world wars and with modernism the defining domestic blueprint, the Lutyenesque house continues to provide us with a vivid illustration of the persistent lure of such dreams.

CONTEXT

Lutyens's houses were built for a specific type of person, at a specific point in time and for specific purposes; and all of these factors had an impact on their design. Most of Lutyens's clients were people who had made their money rather than inherited it and whose titles, if any, were honours bestowed for successful endeavours rather than emblems of an aristocratic pedigree. He largely designed for bankers, stockbrokers, industrialists and businessmen, a class buoyed up on a rising tide of prosperity at the turn of the century. Such people might have aspired to the status of the landed gentry, but held no family estates of their own. As a class, they were also highly vulnerable to political and economic changes; several of Lutyens's clients went bankrupt in succeeding years and many had to drastically curtail their building plans after the introduction of income tax in 1911 dented their fortunes. Money, therefore, was an issue.

By and large, what such clients wanted was a substantial house in the country where they could express and enjoy their prosperity, and where they could entertain. The development of the railway network at the end of the nineteenth century opened up wide possibilities in terms of location. Areas formerly considered too remote were now within easy reach of London or other major cities and for the first time it was practical to commute regularly between town and country on a weekly or even daily basis. The country location was critical: it provided a romantic, traditional counterpoint to the urban life of modern commerce. A consequent requirement for such houses was to provide an expression of rootedness and con-

ABOVE: The garden at Little Thakeham, showing the south-facing oriel window. While the exterior is vernacular, the interior is almost entirely classical.

tinuity. Lutyens, sensing his clients wanted to belong to the settled milieu of gentleman farmers and local squires, designed houses that physically grew out of their contexts and conveyed precisely this degree of security and timelessness. As Miss Jekyll wrote of her house, Munstead Wood:

[it] does not stare with newness; it is not new in any way that is disquieting to the eye; it is neither raw nor callow. On the contrary, it almost gives the impression of a comfortable maturity of something like a couple of hundred years. And yet there is nothing sham or old about it; it is not trumped up with any specious or fashionable devices of spurious antiquity; there is no pretending to be anything that it is not – no affectation whatever.

One way in which Lutyens achieved this sense of continuity in his houses arose from his deliberate employment of different historical elements. A Lutyens house is very rarely completely classical, completely Georgian or completely Tudorbethan in terms of its references. Just as a 400-year-old country manor would have naturally seen many additions and modifications over its lifetime, changes evident in differing styles of exterior and interior elements, Lutyens adopted the same mixed vocabulary in his houses to suggest a wealth of previous traditions woven together in the same location. In lesser hands, such stylistic quotations could have appeared cynical or simply indigestible, but in the case of Lutyens, the references arose from a deep understanding of these traditions and a heartfelt affection for them. Moreover, the elements were generally deployed not as superficial decoration but for a more profound design purpose of which the architect was in complete control. 'By tradition,' Lutyens wrote, 'I do not mean the hanging of Roman togas on Victorian towel-horses. Tradition, to me, consists in our inherited sense of structural fitness, the evolution of rhythmic forms by a synthesis of needs and materials, and the avoidance of arbitrary faults by the exercise of common sense coupled with sensibility.' The distillation of historical elements often serves to create an animating personality. With their tall brick chimneys complementing deep sheltering roofs and

LEFT: *North-facing front of Little Thakeham, which shows a typical sequence of entrances – the gateway, the court and the protected realm of the house itself.*

long horizontal lines of faceted windows, many Lutyens houses, uncannily, seem to have faces. This anthropomorphism derives from Lutyens's humanist sense, placing human needs and human limitations at the centre of his architecture.

Where Lutyens's houses differed from the great country estates of the aristocracy was in the scope of their provision. Many of Lutyens's clients were indeed very wealthy, but few had limitless reserves. Lutyens, in addition, soon acquired a reputation for being an expensive architect, with much of the additional expenses his buildings incurred deriving from architectural features which he felt essential to the integrity of the finished result, but which may not have been

ABOVE: Another entrance sequence at Marshcourt. A bridge leads to a courtyard; the main door opens on to a hallway that leads to the living rooms.

RIGHT: The garden elevations of Lutyens houses were often asymmetric and informal, in contrast to the symmetric formal fronts.

immediately obvious to the client. There was therefore a need for these houses to justify their expense by appearing larger and more substantial than they actually were. It was his great skill as a designer that such aggrandizement rarely resulted in pomposity or bombast.

With the improved communications between metropolitan areas and the countryside, there was no longer the need for country houses to be self-sufficient in terms of produce, as the great estates had been with their home farms and dairies. For this reason, the gardens of Lutyens's houses could be conceived integrally with the architecture, as part of the overall design, and not as necessary productive adjuncts. It is the union between garden and house that so perfectly expresses Lutyens's summary of the English country idyll.

In terms of planning, the typical Lutyens house was designed to facilitate the informality of the weekend house party. To accommodate guests, there were accordingly more bedrooms than one would expect for a family residence, and there were also clear distinctions between public areas for entertaining and receiving guests, and private quarters. At the same time, in common with other houses of the period, there was also a segregation between family members and the domestic staff who waited upon them. Such demarcations were generally achieved in the sequence of movement from area to area, with the

LEFT: Deanery Garden, Lutyens's first commission from Hudson, encapsulates ideals of country living. The link between house and garden was critical.

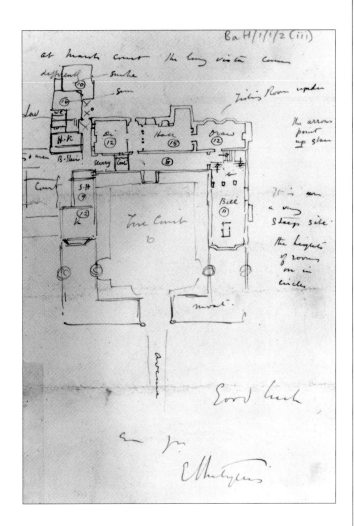

ABOVE: Lutyens's sketch plan of Marshcourt. The indirect layout of routes through and around Lutyens's houses made them seem larger than they actually were.

main reception rooms being interconnected and private enclaves and staff quarters or service rooms clearly separated and sometimes in different wings. Halls, vestibules or galleries were the circulation spaces that served to link all three spheres.

Lutyens's clients were, generally speaking, forward-looking; they wanted tradition, but not at the expense

LEFT: Classical detailing in the Hall at Little Thakeham. The architectural references in Lutyens's houses are rarely of a single period but his mastery of different styles serve to give his work unity.

of modern comforts. Instead of stabling, there was the need to provide garaging for motorcars. Central heating, electric power and indoor plumbing were all conveniences that were increasingly expected. Lutyens, predictably, went to some lengths to prevent such mundanities from interrupting his architectural effects. At Marshcourt, for example, garaging was provided in one barn, with an electric generator for the house in another – 'With this architect everything and everyone has a house,' wrote Jane Brown in *Lutyens and the Edwardians*. Lutyens was particularly keen on an elevational detail which concealed guttering behind a parapet; less practically, he had a tendency to run servicing within the masonry construction of walls, an arrangement which has had the subsequent effect of making such systems difficult to maintain and update.

Wherever possible, Lutyens sited his houses so that the main reception rooms faced south, where they provided easy access to the garden. This arrangement arose directly out of the principal purpose of these houses as places for enjoyment and entertainment. The whole point of taking the trouble to build in the countryside was to promote a connection with nature and the type of outdoor recreation impossible in the city. With a south-facing aspect making the best site for gardens in a northern climate, this natural orientation contributed a great deal to the sense of ease and grace of the overall designs. The north side of the houses, accordingly, was where main entrances were typically located.

Lutyens expressed the difference between the formal front and informal back in his elevational treatments. Although his early houses were generally asymmetric in arrangement, with the main entrance often located at the side, rather than the front, in his later works, symmetry and regularity came to dominate the public aspect of his houses, with their entrances achieved through a sequence of carefully modulated approaches. At the rear, the elevation was much less formal, with living areas extending out into the garden by means of terraces and changes of level. This, however, was not a question of blurring the boundary between inside and out; if anything, it was a case of extending the boundary, so that the whole house and garden became part of the same protected domain. In this sense, every house Lutyens designed was a castle, an enclave, and a powerful fulfilment of the wishes and aspirations of his clients. They were, and are, worlds in miniature.

MATERIAL QUALITY

One of the defining characteristics of Lutyens's houses is his evocative use of materials, both to ground buildings in their local context and to provide contrasts of texture that help to articulate form. Local materials, traditionally worked, were a marked feature of his early houses in Surrey. Lutyens had a particular knowledge and love of wood, especially oak, which he used externally, internally and in his furniture designs. This expressive use of materials was dependent, not only on his own sympathy and expertise, but on the continuing existence of a good skill base. Like the village carpenter who taught the young Lutyens how to tell when an oak was ready for felling by the taste of the acorn, in country areas

Above: Detail of materials used at Marshcourt: white chalk inset with red tiles and grey flints.

around the turn of the century there were still many such craftsmen, whose working methods had been handed down from generation to generation. In many Lutyens houses, there was ample scope for such craftsmen to display their virtuosity – in architectural details such as the carving of balustrades, the intricate twisted brickwork of tall chimneystacks or the flourish of decorative plasterwork.

The use of local materials was an important way in which Lutyens expressed sensitivity to context. Stone quarried in the vicinity, bricks handmade from local clay, wood felled and seasoned no more than a few miles from where it would be worked, provided an inbuilt harmony which rooted buildings to their site. The truthful employment of natural, local materials was an important element of the Arts and Crafts approach, to which Lutyens, especially in the early part of his career, wholeheartedly subscribed.

In this context, it is worth looking in greater detail at Munstead Wood, the house Lutyens designed for Gertrude Jekyll, a commission more in the nature of a collaboration. The house was built of Bargate stone, a local sandstone, with tiled roofs, tall brick chimneys

BELOW: Detail from the staircase at basement level at Marshcourt. Lutyens used combinations of materials to provide rhythm and texture.

and casement windows framed in oak. All the materials were of local origin. Since Miss Jekyll extensively documented the process of creating Munstead Wood, it is possible to build up a detailed picture of the thinking behind the design. In *Home and Garden* she wrote:

The architect has a thorough knowledge of the local ways of using the sandstone that grows in our hills, and that for many centuiries has been the building material of the district, and of all the lesser incidental methods of adapting means to ends that mark the well-defined way of building of the coun-

try, so that what he builds seems to grow naturally out of the ground. I always think it a pity to use in any one place the distinctive methods of another. Every part of the country has its own traditional ways, and if these have in the course of many centuries become 'crystallised' into any particular form we may be sure that there is some good reason for it, and it follows that the attempt to use the ways and methods of some distant place is sure to give an impression as of something uncomfortably exotic, of geographical confusion, of the perhaps right thing in the wrong place.

In another long passage, which is worth quoting in full, she goes on to explain the special depth of character that comes from using materials from a local and living source:

There is the actual living interest of knowing where the trees one's house is built of really grew. The three great beams, ten inches square, that stretch across the ceiling of the sitting-room, and do other work besides, and bear up a good part of the bedroom space above (they are twenty-eight foot long), were growing fifteen years ago a mile and a half away, on the outer edge of a fir wood just above a hazel-fringed hollow lane, whose steep sandy sides, here and there level enough to bear a patch of vegetation, grew tall Bracken and great Foxgloves, and the finest wild Canterbury Bells I ever saw. At the top of the western bank, their bases hidden in cool beds of tall Fern in summer, and clothed in its half-fallen warmth of rusty com-

fort in winter, and in spring-time standing on their carpet of blue wild Hyacinth, were these tall oaks; one or two of their fellows still remain. Often driving up the lane from early childhood I used to see these great grey trees, in twilight looking almost ghostly against the darkly-mysterious background of the sombre firs. And I remember always thinking how straight and tall they looked, for these sandy hills do not readily grow such great oaks as are found in the clay weald a few miles to the south and at the foot of our warm-soiled hills. But I am glad to know that my beams are these same old friends, and that the pleasure that I had in watching them green and growing is not destroyed but only changed as I see them stretching above me as grand beams of solid English oak.

Much later, in 1932, when Lutyens was invited to answer questions at an informal meeting at the Architectural Association, he was asked for his views on the use of steel and concrete. His reply goes a long way to explaining why he never embraced modern materials:

I enjoy all construction, and the steel girder with its petticoat of concrete is a most useful ally in the ever-recurring advent of difficulty. The thin walls are worth while, if only to watch your Client's face

RIGHT: *Miss Jekyll's house, Munstead Wood, seems to grow naturally out of its surroundings, which is all the more remarkable since it was built in what was already a mature garden.*

ABOVE: Deanery Garden is constructed of red Berkshire brick – the site was already enclosed by an old brick wall. In the vaulted entrance passage, however, white chalk is introduced to make a graphic banding.

glow with joy at winning a few square feet of carpet. But I crave for the soft thick noiseless walls of hand-made brick and lime, the deep light-reflecting reveals, the double floors, easy stairways, and doorways never less than one foot six inches from a corner … The time may come when we shall be able to choose girders to our taste, as we select particular boughs of particular oaks for struts and braces. Then will girders become friendly and personal.

As this passage reveals, Lutyens appreciated materials in the fullest sense, for the special qualities they could bring to a building. 'You cannot go far wrong in building-colour if you use local materials,' he said. Natural materials mellow with time, they age sympathetically, acquiring a patina of use which gives charm and character to a house. At the same time, varying materials allows contrasts of texture to come into play, contrasts that may be bold and graphic or operate on a more subtle level. As Christopher Hussey writes: 'Texture is not architecture; but architecture is not wholly successful without it.'

At Orchards, the home he built for the Chances just a mile or so from Munstead Wood, Lutyens again used the local sandstone, set off with tiles around archways and over windows. Oak was employed to frame the casement windows and the gable of the porch.

For Goddards, further east in the Surrey Hills, the medley of materials was less mellow but equally picturesque: roughcast whitewashed walls contrasting with red brick mullioned windows and tiled roofs, covered in dark Horsham slate lower down.

ABOVE: The entranceway to the courtyard at Orchards is reminiscent of an old coaching inn. The roof is supported by curved oak brackets.

Away from Surrey, Lutyens displayed the same instinctive handling of local materials. Deanery Garden, built for his friend Edward Hudson, was planned within a walled garden on the banks of the Thames at Sonning, a village near Reading. It features the red Berkshire brick of the area, combined with

LEFT: *The entrance vestibule at Marshcourt, where ornate decorative plasterwork mouldings constrast with the austerity of the chalk walls.*

ABOVE: *The chalk base of the billiard table at Marshcourt is evidence of Lutyens's playful use of materials.*

tile and timber to create, in the words of Christopher Hussey, 'a perfect architectural sonnet'. An existing old brick wall, running up from the river to the village high street, provided the starting point to the design and the house is sited to fit right up against it. A vaulted passage leading from the main entrance, which is directly off the road, features the contrasting use of chalk and brick in bold geometric banding.

But it is at Marshcourt in Hampshire, begun in 1901, where Lutyens was to display a truly virtuoso use of materials. He had been commissioned by Herbert Johnson, a stockbroker, to build him a house at Stockbridge, overlooking the River Test. The dramatic effect of Marshcourt relies on the daring use of chalk for the main construction. Chalk or 'clunch' had been a common building material in the Middle Ages and was much used in the vaulting of churches, but although it is very strong in compression, capable of taking great loads, it had fallen out of common use. Lutyens had a particular affection for chalk downlands and his choice of clunch for Marshcourt enabled him virtually to sculpt a house out of its landscape. In addition, the chalk allowed him to achieve a graphic whiteness in the building without recourse to applied finishes such as whitewash: it was thus a choice in perfect accordance with those Arts and Crafts principles of honesty. Lawrence Weaver, editor of *Country Life* and chronicler of Lutyens's career, describes the effect (in *Houses and Gardens by E.L. Lutyens*):

The house seeks its effect by ingenious combinations of local materials, by sharp contrasts of colour – white chalk, black flint and red brick – by daring groupings and by the juxtaposition of features of varying scales. Experience shows that such a conception, unless handled in a bold and masterly way, is bound to fail from the lack of that essential unity which is needed in any perfected work of art; but Mr Lutyens has essayed a *tour de force*, and achieved it.

The same chalk is employed indoors at Marshcourt to form the plinth of the billiard table in the billiard room – 'to chalk your cue' was the playful, and perhaps inevitable, Lutyens pun.

The early part of Lutyens career, when he was designing in the 'picturesque' mode, provides the most striking examples of sensitive combinations of materials. But even when he grew to favour treatments which expressed a more dominant use of a single material, Lutyens was never indifferent to locality. The stonework of Heathcote places the house firmly in its Yorkshire context but a dour effect was avoided by the use of tiling for the roofs, instead of slate in the local tradition. The austere stone of Lindisfarne, whose internal stairs and corridors seem hewn from the rock, is at one with its rocky site off the Northumbrian coast.

The massive granite blocks from which Castle Drogo is constructed are entirely right for both the type of building and the rugged nature of its

RIGHT: A harmonious combination of materials announces a doorway at Grey Walls, Scotland (1900). Cream rubble walls are inset with tiles, used edge-on.

Right: Looking north below the entry tower at Castle Drogo. The building is constructed of massive granite blocks, a sympathetic choice for a rugged location on the edge of Dartmoor.

Dartmoor setting. The castle's asymmetry, however, which gives it more of an organic appearance than that of his other work of the period (the last stone on this long-term project was not laid until 1925), was not deliberate: what was built represents only one-third of the initial projected design. One reason for the curtailment of the scheme was the decision of his client, J.C. Drewe, to have the walls doubled in thickness, a decision which naturally increased the cost. The power of the castle rests on its rigorous logic: it is not a building in fancy dress. As Christopher Hussey remarks: 'The ultimate justification of Drogo is that it does not pretend to be a castle. It *is* a castle, as a castle is built, of granite, on a mountain, in the twentieth century.'

In contrast, the elegant use of brickwork set off with crisp white painted sash windows epitomizes the gentle Wrennaissance style displayed in houses such as Ednaston Manor in Derbyshire and The Salutation on the Kent coast. Lutyens adored brick and was particularly fond of a narrow two-inch variety, laid with wide mortar bonds.

The same sympathetic treatment of materials continued indoors, with many materials used both externally and internally to create an effect of simplicity, rigour and honesty. This recurring use of materials is looked at in more detail in the next chapter, but in this context it is worth pointing out that Lutyens's vocabulary of materials could be put to subtle uses in his interior planning to signal progression and movement through spaces. What happened underfoot, surfaces that barely registered consciously as brick, tile or stone that gave way to oak, were

employed to announce different areas of the house. Sometimes, particularly in his later work, he used surprisingly successful contrasts of grand and humble materials to provide contrasts of colour and texture. One of the most striking examples occurred at Heathcote. The floor of the vestibule, the immediate point of entry to the house, was paved in white marble, an expected choice for a classical building. But inset in the floor were panels composed of brick laid in a herringbone fashion, a domestic echo of those early vernacular houses.

ORCHESTRATING SPACE

In the modern idiom, derived from Le Corbusier, it has been accepted that the plan is the generator of architectural form, in other words that one begins with the functional disposition of spaces and from this arrangement the three-dimensional building follows. 'Form follows function' is the neat encapsulation of the theory: start with what the building needs to provide, and the rest follows logically.

Lutyens, who reviewed the seminal work in which these views were first expressed, Le Corbusier's *Towards a New Architecture* (1923), did not disagree about the importance of the plan. He did, however, disagree about its pre-eminence. For Lutyens, the plan represented only one of architecture's three critical dimensions. As a child, Lutyens had begun his unorthodox architectural education by studying local

RIGHT: The entrance hall at Lindisfarne is a complex space, divided in three by thick columns and rounded arches. The columns seem to grow up from the floor.

Left: The dining room in the London house of Candia Lutyens and Paul Peterson. The use of rounded arches flanking a fireplace are a typical Lutyens device for increasing the sense of space. The Spiderback chairs were made to an original Lutyens design, as was the 'cardinal's hat' light fitting, which was first designed for Campion Hall.

buildings with the aid of his viewing glass and tracing round the three-dimensional forms. For the rest of his life, he conceived a building three-dimensionally first and then worked out the plan. This is not to say that his plans were not functional expressions of the needs of a household, or logical in themselves, simply that he did not reduce architecture to mere functionality: 'Architecture, with its love and passion, begins where function ends,' he wrote.

Because Lutyens thought primarily in terms of volumes of space, not in plans, nor in flat façades or elevations, his buildings provide a richness of spatial experience. There is contrast – small, low spaces that give on to large, high ones – and there are also views and vistas that do not reveal the whole at once but provide sudden glimpses from odd places.

In a recent article, *Metiendo Vivendum:* "By Measure We Must Live" (Achitectural Research Quarterly, vol. 3, no. 2, 1999), John Rollo has published the results of an analysis of 40 ground-floor plans of Lutyens's houses. Rollo's study demonstrates that Lutyens consistently used ratios to structure his work, notably the golden section, and ratios based on a Fibonacci progression: 1:1:2:3:5:8. In Rollo's view, Lutyens's use of such ratios was not necessarily preconceived, but derived naturally from the fact that he drew up his designs on 1/8th-inch squared paper. In support of this theory he quotes an extract from a talk by Oswald Milne, one of Lutyens's apprentices (*The AA Journal*, March 1959) in which Milne describes how the design for Little Thakeham came about. Lutyens had persuaded the client that the house should be built in stone rather than brick:

When he got back to London that evening he handed me two sheets of squared paper – he liked to use squared paper – with this house, Little Thakeham, almost completely worked out in sketch form, with all the plans, sections and elevations. He must have done the whole thing in the train ... Little Thakeham as built is almost exactly to the sketch which he made in that way.

The use of proportional ratios enabled Lutyens to combine symmetrical facades with asymmetrical plans: it permitted a certain element of freedom within a framework of control. As Rollo explains: 'Exploring with contrasting and localized symmetries, shifting axes and a wide range of movement patterns, Lutyens was able to invoke varying perceptions of enlargement, surprise and enticement.'

Even when at his most classical, Lutyens rarely adopted a symmetrical spatial arrangement, with a hierarchical progression from entrance to hall to reception room. The symmetry of plan common to eighteenth-century houses had its roots in a formality of living which derived from the stately pattern of a royal palace. Rooms were arranged on a main axis, with each progressive space, as ante-room succeeded ante-room, approaching the ultimate goal, the seat of power.

By contrast, even when Lutyens's houses looked classical, they did not feel classical to live in. The Edwardian preference was for informality, charm and domesticity, not the expression of authority. At the same time, there was a vogue for the 'living hall', a romantic adaptation of the medieval 'hall house' whose central space accommodated the majority of domestic activities. In either of his two principal modes, vernacular or classical, Lutyens planned his houses so that all was not immediately apparent, and so that moving through the different spaces was at least as enjoyable as eventual arrival.

This progression would typically begin with the approach to the house. The visitor, passing through entry gates, sometimes flanked by lodges, would cross a forecourt before reaching the house proper. At this point, there might be a porch sheltering the substantial and reassuring main door. This entrance would in turn give on to a vestibule or corridor running parallel to the frontage which it would be necessary to traverse before reaching the main Hall. The Hall, in turn, formed part of an interconnecting suite of reception rooms and thus offered a choice of direction. The transverse vestibule or corridor was often repeated on the first floor, sometimes in the form of a gallery.

Such sequences of movement served important purposes. By arranging routes so that they went the long way round, rather than travelled the shortest distance between two points, Lutyens was able to multiply spatial experiences and thus make a house seem bigger than it actually was. He was also able to set up surprises, whose theatricality similarly served to enhance the perception of space. In this context, the large proportion of area devoted to stairs, halls,

RIGHT: Lutyens was profligate with circulation space, as shown by the staircase at Marshcourt. The effect was to multiply views from level to level and make houses seem bigger than they in fact were.

LEFT: The hall at Marshcourt, looking east towards the dining room. The elaborate decorative frieze above the archway is carved from chalk.

RIGHT: Looking west through the hall screen; the hall itself connects the dining room with the drawing room. The ceiling is ornamented with Jacobean style plasterwork.

ABOVE: *The gallery at Munstead Wood. Glass-fronted china cupboards face casement windows on the other side. Miss Jekyll chose the bedroom at the far end because she enjoyed walking along the gallery.*

LEFT: *The main stairs to the dining room at Castle Drogo are dramatically lit by vertical windows to accentuate the height of the space.*

vestibules, landings and corridors in the typical Lutyens house, far from representing a wasteful indulgence, actually sets up rhythms which animate the entire building. It was, as he wrote, 'the waste of space that, unwittingly, creates that most valuable asset, a gain of space.' At The Salutation, for example, one of Lutyens's smaller houses, a third of the entire volume is taken up by a grand staircase arranged around a void. From a modern point of view, the generosity of the stair, not to mention the empty void it surrounds, is sheer extravagance, yet it contributes immeasurably to the pleasure and delight of the architecture.

Munstead Wood is an early example of Lutyens providing this degree of enjoyment through movement. One of the house's most celebrated features is the first floor gallery which runs along the north side of the house. The gallery, floored in oak and framed by oak posts and beams, is lit on one side by long casement windows and fitted out on the other with glass-fronted oak cupboards designed to accommodate Miss Jekyll's many treasures. The gallery is reached via the main stair which rises from the hall below; at its far end is the bedroom which Miss Jekyll chose as her own, simply to have the daily pleasure of walking the length of the gallery. Of the gallery, Miss Jekyll wrote:

> ... it is a part of the house that gives me so much pleasure, and it meets with so much approval from those whose knowledge and taste I most respect, that I venture to describe it in terms of admiration. Thanks to my good architect, who conceived the place in exactly such a form as I had desired, but could not have described, and the fine old carpen-

RIGHT: The South Main Staircase at Viceroy's House has no roof so that air can circulate, but there is a deep coving surrounding the open ceiling. As the stair was generally used after dark, the effect was to create a 'ceiling' of stars.

ter who worked to his drawings in an entirely sympathetic manner, I may say that it is a good example of how English oak should be used in an honest building … And because the work has been planned and executed in this spirit, this gallery, and indeed the whole house, has that quality – the most valuable to my thinking that a house or any part of it can possess – of conducing to respose and serenity of mind. In some mysterious way it is imbued with an expression of cheerful, kindly welcome, of restfulness to mind and body, of abounding satisfaction to eye and brain.

Another spatial device which Lutyens used extensively to increase the apparent size of his houses was to arrange the plan around open courtyards, unbuilt areas whose volume contributed to the overall impression of scale. Lutyens generally had reasonably generous sites with which to work and his houses typically occupied a significant degree of ground area, with L-shaped or H-shaped plans extending to frame or enclose these open spaces of court and garden. The inevitable result, however, was that with proportionately so much more surface area to construct than might be expected from the amount of accommodation actually provided, Lutyens's houses generally proved very expensive.

The rhythm of alternating open and enclosed areas is at its finest in Viceroy's House. The demands of the climate, necessitating a free flow of air to cool the interior, allowed Lutyens to achieve his most complex interpenetration of spaces, with rooms accessed from loggias arranged around internal courtyards.

Some of Lutyens's most magical sequences were achieved here. The state staircase leading up to the state rooms and the Durbar Hall was generally only used after dark on formal occasions such as balls and banquets. Accordingly, it has no roof, but a deep curved cove creates the suggestion of a ceiling, framing the starry night. On each landing on the grand staircase there are low basins of water built into the turn of the stairs and lined in black marble, mysterious pools that both cool the air and conjure up the romance of Mogul water gardens.

Music, of all the arts, comes closest to architecture. Both have strong foundations in mathematics, both have rhythms, harmonies and themes, and both are notoriously hard to describe in words. Elisabeth, Lutyens's third daughter, became a noted composer. During a time in the 1920s when she kept house for her father, the two grew close. In an article published in 1926 Lutyens wrote: 'All great periods of architecture have one common and essential denominator: Unity in the measured tread of their rhythms; nothing left to chance. Method, Scale, Rhythm, based on realities and observed with the rigidity of Music, are necessities to all great architecture … Architecture, like music, requires an orchestra of many men and instruments.' On another occasion, he stated, 'My generation believed that the measure of man's architecture was man, and that the rhythm of a building should correspond to the rhythms familiar in human

RIGHT: The grandeur of the Durbar Hall in Viceroy's House is accentuated by the dramatic geometric floor design executed in black and white marble.

life. All architecture must have rhythms that affect the eye, as music does the ear …' As Elisabeth Lutyens later recorded in her memoir, *A Goldfish Bowl*, Lutyens was 'fascinated and excited at the realization that music was built on structural principles and relationships stemming, as did architecture, from the Greeks'.

Lutyens's orchestration of space, with its rhythmic sequences, counterpoints and crescendos could not be further removed from the functional reductionism that states a building must be generated by the plan. His houses were never cost-effective and his way of building died out with the last generation who could afford it. The loss, as he foresaw, was a certain loss of poetry in architecture.

LIGHT

'Light is the most important element that architects have to compose with,' said Lutyens. Space cannot be orchestrated without light – or more specifically, without light's partner, shadow. Light and shade delineate form and affect perception of volume. How light is admitted to the interior, the disposition of windows and other openings, is no less important. And with such openings comes the whole issue of views.

Lutyens had an acute understanding of light in architecture and very specific ways of treating windows in his buildings. Most importantly, he understood that light is inherently variable. Unlike many other architects, who treated light as an even source coming from a single direction, Lutyens had a full appreciation of its subtleties. 'Those idiotic diagrams which architects and others make don't work,'

he wrote. 'Light is a flood, and you might as well try to show the banks of a river, its flow and varying depths, swirls, eddies, and currents with one arrow.' His sensitivity to context also expressed itself in his handling of light. Very different strategies were employed in the harsh, glaring conditions of the Indian sun than were adopted in the gentle, muted daylight of the English countryside. 'Our climate is the architect's colour and he must acknowledge it, play up to it,' said Lutyens.

One of Lutyens's darker houses was Munstead Wood, which was lit atmospherically but rather dimly. Nevertheless, Munstead Wood is not lacking in windows. In his earlier vernacular houses, Lutyens often used windows to express a strong horizontal element. At Munstead Wood, as at other examples from this period, low casement windows were used in almost continuous bands on different storeys. Occasionally, a line of windows would wrap around a corner: Lutyens appreciated the liveliness of light coming from two directions. Jane Brown, author of *Lutyens and the Edwardians,* lived in Goddards for a year. The house has the same small windows as Munstead Wood and she observed the special quality of light that Lutyens was able to achieve in his interiors:

Every day becomes a theatrical performance of light changes and values, and the house picks up on this. One becomes accustomed to seeing the late afternoon sun slanting on a particular streak of flowered Donegal carpet; one constructs the day according to the sunlight in the rooms or the shady

RIGHT: *View along the upper corridor at Marshcourt. The corridor is oak-panelled and lined with cupboards for linen. Open joists are typically 'honest' in the Arts and Crafts manner, but equally important as a means of introducing slivers of light to offset the darkness of the timber.*

corners in the heat of the day. The light becomes a companion, ever shifting, completely reflecting the seasons and time of the day, with no need of a clock.

The typical orientation of a Lutyens house, with main reception and living rooms located to the south, made the most of natural light in a climate where grey skies are often the norm. But he also exploited the special qualities of light coming from other directions, notably the golden tints of the setting sun. As Miss Jekyll describes her sitting room: 'A long low range of window lights it from the south, and in the afternoon a flood of western light streams down the stairs from another long window on the middle landing … The windows, after the manner of the best old buildings of the country, are set with their oak mullions flush with the outer face of the wall, so that as the wall is of a good thickness, every window has a broad oak window-board, eighteen inches wide.' Lady Chance's studio at Orchards, where she worked on her sculpture, is practically lit by a large north-facing bay window.

The 'window-board' or reveal was one of Lutyens's strategies for creating a gentle diffusion of light rather than a harsh glare. 'Deep window reveals which reflect, distributing a diffused light, give the most kindly illumination,' according to Lutyens. The case-ment window, set in the thickness of the wall, was a feature of many Arts and Crafts houses. The deep reveal, which had such a beneficial effect on the qual-ity of light, also expressed the constructional integrity of the building. Many of Lutyens's clients also appre-ciated the consequent generosity of the sills, which provided surfaces for plants and ornaments.

The casement windows at Munstead Wood were the occasion for an altercation between client and architect. The range of windows comprised individ-ual casements and Lutyens wanted the ones next to the end to be the opening casements. Miss Jekyll, on the other hand, wanted the end casements to open, and she won. Later, she regretted making her archi-tect go against his better judgement. With the end casements open, rain could soak the curtains or wind blow them out untidily.

Another feature of casement windows is their com-position of faceted panes of glass or leaded lights. In Elizabethan times, there were good practical reasons for such an arrangement. Glass could not be manu-factured in very large sizes and piecing small individual panes together was the only way to achieve

RIGHT: *The small leaded casement windows at Munstead Wood are typical features of Lutyens's designs in the vernacular idiom. The many facets of glass provide a sparkling sense of animation on the exterior.*

LEFT: *Light streams through three tiers of casements wrapped around a bay in the hall at Marshcourt. Unlike picture windows, which can have a rather static quality, the many subdivisions of the casement add vitality to views.*

a larger opening. At the end of the nineteenth century, such practical limitations had long been overcome and, while plate glass was still in the future, there was no technical reason for filling windows with leaded lights. The casement, as a vernacular element, was used for purely picturesque purposes in the Arts and Crafts aesthetic; in the twentieth century, countless poorly wrought suburban variations on the theme have since made such features very hackneyed indeed. But one value of the casement window pattern, which Lutyens was quick to appreciate, was that it avoided the blank glare of a larger area of glass. 'Glass as an essential material has to be used, but I prefer its use in moderate sizes and faceted so no sheet of glare is produced,' said Lutyens. 'Areas of glass alone do not give serviceable light.' In recent times, this has become increasingly appreciated. Large picture windows, as Christopher Alexander has pointed out in *The Pattern Language*, can have a curiously deadening effect on an interior: a view which is ever-present and uninterrupted has a dull, static quality.

The facets of casement windows also produce a lively aspect on the outside of the building. Catching and reflecting the light, their glinting surfaces animate the façades of houses, making a sparkling contrast to brick and timber. Particularly dramatic were the strong vertical contrasts of double-height oriel windows, composed like the casements of individual small panes, but rising up to announce the great public rooms they lit.

In his later houses, Lutyens abandoned the casement pattern more or less totally in favour of the

LEFT: The south-facing oriel window at Little Thakeham bathes the interior with warm light. Lutyens took particular care over the orientation of his buildings.

RIGHT: The kitchen at Castle Drogo is in a basement. A glazed rotundo, based on Soane's design for the Bank of England, provides essential top lighting.

classic Georgian sash. But although the style of window was different, the effect was similar. Sash windows, neatly subdivided into panes, provide the same faceted aspect as casements but on a more generous scale. Lutyens was fanatical about the ratios expressed in such subdivisions, as one of his architectural assistants recalled: 'There were certain elementary rules which, once seized, had to be applied throughout the whole building or composition. For example, all window panes had to be identical in proportion, generally in that of a square to its diagonal in height.' These white painted sashes, expressing such mathematical rigour, provided a tautness to classical or Wrennaissance elevations. Occasionally, they also provided a means for architectural surprise, their regularity and even placement disguising different internal volumes.

With many of his houses enclosing, at least partially, open courts, Lutyens was able to draw more light into the interior and set up more dynamic views and vistas than a more conventional plan would allow. Unlike the dreary shaft of a light well, punched through the centre of a tall block, such central open spaces had their own light-filled vitality which infused the spirit of the house.

Windows were not the only means of playing with light in the interior. Lutyens, like an earlier English architect who delighted in surprise and wit, Sir John Soane, was adept at the use of mirror to multiply the effects of light and views. One characteristic Lutyens strategy was to place a fireplace in the corner of a room, with a mirror above reflecting through 90 degrees. Another was to use mirror to complete a

symmetry. The classical addition of a ballroom to Marshcourt features mirrored 'windows' along the internal wall in exact duplication of the real windows on the other side.

But in many Lutyens buildings, light also pops up in odd places, almost as a tease. At Marshcourt, again, open joists in the staircase provide the merest of glimpses, slivers and patches of light whose role in adding to the overall level of illumination is minimal. There is characteristic Arts and Crafts 'honesty' about the expression of the construction, but the sudden unexpected views in the sequence of movement from level to level are pure Lutyens.

COURT AND GARDEN

'A garden scheme should have a backbone, a central idea beautifully phrased. Every wall, path, stone and flower should have its relationship to the central idea,' said Lutyens. Lutyens is one of the rare architects whose buildings cannot be considered in isolation from their surroundings. Site, for any designer of houses, is always important but, in Lutyens' work, house and garden were conceived as a whole. Often working in collaboration with Gertrude Jekyll, Lutyens was able to achieve 'houses for gardens and gardens for houses'.

Just how connected were Lutyens's houses and gardens can be judged from the fact that he went to great lengths to arrange internal planning to provide views. The views *from* the house were just as important as the views *of* the house; 'the position of the staircase window may materially affect the garden plan; so may the manner in which the vertical face of the

Right: Gertrude Jekyll in her garden at Munstead Wood, aged 80. Lutyens and Miss Jekyll were able to create 'houses for gardens and gardens for houses'.

house is attached by design to the garden …' Lutyens had a profound understanding of gardening; its implicit commitment to the future, its expression of time and continuity.

The word 'garden' is particularly significant. The houses that Lutyens designed for his well-to-do clients may have been set in substantial grounds by today's standards, but they were very far from being country estates. There was no need for these sites to be productive, to provide income from managed farms or supply food for the table. What was required, instead, were miniature Edens that evoked the whole spirit of living close to nature – together with enough land for those country recreations of shooting and fishing. The intimate connection between house and garden was not merely to do with physical arrangement, or providing easy transition between indoors and out. The connection was the whole point. The consequent unity virtually defined the idea of the country house. According to Vita Sackville-West the ideal country house is 'essentially part of the country, not only *in* the country but part of it, a natural growth'.

As architectural critic Peter Inskip has pointed out, Lutyens clearly expressed the importance of the garden in his architectural planning. In his earliest work, the hall is treated as the most significant space, in keeping with the Edwardian concept of the 'living

LEFT *Walkway under a pergola at Marshcourt. Lutyens conceived gardens architecturally, with a series of 'rooms' connected by paths and changes in level.*

hall'. Gradually, however, in subsequent houses, the hall is pushed back further into the house so that it is no longer just the focus of the building, but the focus of the site as a whole. Eventually, in later works, Lutyens treats the garden terrace immediately adjoining the house as the ultimate destination or climax of the plan. The house is far from incidental, but it plays an essentially supporting role. The garden is the most private of spaces in the hierarchy, while the house serves as its entry point.

This type of planning reinforces both a romantic idea of the countryside and a sense of ownership. The garden does not merely serve as an attractive or picturesque attachment to the house, providing pleasant views or somewhere to take a relaxing stroll; it acts as a protectorate, a domain, a place set apart and secure from the outside world. Lutyens's houses and gardens very explicitly state that an Englishman's home is his castle.

Lutyens structured his gardens in a similar way to his houses, as a sequence of 'rooms' or courts connected by walkways and changes of level. While the notion of the garden as 'outdoor room' is commonplace today and generally implies a furnished, domestic extension of living areas indoors, for Lutyens the idea was more architectural. Boundaries and changes in level were an important means of

RIGHT: Pergola at Little Thakeham leading away from the house. The strong architectural lines of Lutyens's gardens are softened by naturalistic planting, a style that Gertrude Jekyll helped to popularize.

implying distinct garden areas and of setting up a progression from place to place. The walls of such outdoor rooms might be composed of hedging, planting or actual built walls of different heights. 'Corridors' were often formed by walkways shaded by pergolas. Sunken gardens, with a sheet of water the lowest-lying element, also provided a sense of

ABOVE: Lutyens carried out extensions and alterations to Folly Farm, Berkshire over a considerable period. Water was a common feature of his garden designs.

enclosure. Lutyens particularly loved water – fishing was his only outdoor recreation – and many of his gardens include pools, tanks or narrow canals or strips of water. The Sunk Pool Garden at Marshcourt is one of the more famous examples, while at Folly Farm, Berkshire, originally a small farm cottage, extended twice by Lutyens, the robust form of a loggia or brick-built cloister adjoining the dining room was reflected in a tank or pool.

BELOW: Detail of the stone steps descending to the formal garden at Folly Farm. They begin semi-circular and end as a full circle.

Formality and symmetry were a marked feature of Lutyens's garden designs, with main axis routes providing views and vistas and a strong controlling element. Pavilions were used as counterpoints to the main house and served as places of destination. Sculptural features – sundials were a favourite – acted as punctuation points. There were characteristic Lutyenesque details: walls topped with ridge tiles, spirals executed in brick stone, flights of steps which began as semi-circles and ended in perfect circles,

ABOVE: A water-filled stone trough at Hestercombe, Somerset (1904). This 'canal', with its loop pools, is part of an extensive formal layout.

RIGHT: A pedimented alcove at Hestercombe, with stone steps softened by planting. Materials are local in origin, which adds to the natural effect.

bridges over dry moats, brick or tile extravagantly laid on edge to provide a textural interruption in paving. There were almost never conservatories: the Victorian fascination for glass houses filled with exotic specimens had given way to the Edwardian instinct for naturalism.

Boundaries of the site as a whole were sometimes obviously marked out by walls or hedging or even dry moats, sometimes implied by a falling away of levels. The overall effect was to distance both house and garden from its surroundings: nature in its raw untamed state was not allowed to come up to the back door, but was viewed, picturesquely at a distance, from carefully managed vantage points.

What makes these gardens so quintessentially English, however, arose out of Lutyens's creative collaboration with Gertrude Jekyll. Miss Jekyll was one of the first English gardeners to promote naturalistic planting and she is generally credited as singlehandedly reviving the traditional cottage garden. She wrote:

No artificial planting can ever equal that of Nature, but one may learn from it (i.e. Nature) the great lesson of the importance of moderation and reserve, of simplicity of intention, of directness of purpose, and the inestimable value of the quality

LEFT: The rose arbour at Hestercombe features a timber pergola supported by piers made of local rubble stone. The piers are arranged to frame views of a sundial at the centre of a diagonal arrangement of grass pathways.

called 'breadth' in painting. For planting ground is painting a landscape with living things. *(Wood and Garden)*

Gertrude Jekyll, having had her artistic life as a painter curtailed by deteriorating eyesight, turned only in her forties to the garden as her canvas. Her painter's eye led her to use plants in drifts of colour to form a whole, balanced composition:

I am strongly of the opinion that the possession of a quantity of plants, however good the plants may be in themselves and however ample their number, does not make a great garden; it only makes a *collection*. Having got the plants, the great thing is to use them with careful selection and definite intention. Merely having them, or having them planted unassorted in garden spaces, is only like having a box of paints from the best colourman, or, to go on one step further, it is like having portions of these paints set out upon a palette.

Gertrude Jekyll designed most of the planting for Lutyens gardens up until the turn of the century, but carried on working in collaboration with him for thirty years – she died only in 1932. In the great gardens she and Lutyens made together, where the formality of the basic structure, its architecture, is softened by the naturalistic style of planting, they represent a hugely successful marriage of two traditions. As Lutyens put it, 'No artist has so wide a palette as the garden designer, and no artist greater need of discretion and reserve.'

THREE

TASTE

The Lutyenesque house, for all its variety of historical influence, and with all of its richness of spatial experience, displays a profound unity of design. This is hardly surprising since Lutyens conceived not only interior and exterior spaces, but also internal decorative schemes, architectural detail, furniture and fittings for many of his houses. One reason for revisiting the Lutyens legacy is the opportunity it provides to look in closer detail at his schemes for interior decoration and furnishing, an area of his work that has often been sidestepped in favour of his architectural achievements. Lutyens had a rigorous approach to design; his attention to detail is integral to his architecture. Full of character and personality, such interior schemes are profoundly in sympathy with traditional features without in any way representing a 'period style'.

Lutyens excelled at divining a client's wishes and interpreting their requirements; equally, he excelled at persuading clients to accept his own particular vision when their tastes did not precisely coincide with his own. At Heathcote, where the client originally wanted an oak staircase, Lutyens insisted on marble, and got his way: 'Heathcote', wrote Christopher Hussey, 'is the outstanding example of a client thus getting the exact opposite of what he originally wanted, down to the smallest detail, and becoming immensely proud of it.'

The result of this degree of control was that Lutyens's houses have a distinctive flavour, an evanescent quality which is difficult to define. One of the Baring children, for whose family Lutyens had enlarged and renovated Lambay Castle in Ireland, said that it was always possible to identify Lutyens's houses because they 'smelled the same'. Lutyens's daughter Mary, who spent some time recuperating at Munstead Wood a year after Gertrude Jekyll died, remembered that it still smelled evocatively of new wood. Richard Hannay, John Buchan's fictional cre-

RIGHT: The Ship Room at Lindisfarne Castle, converted by Lutyens from one of the gunpowder magazines of the old fort.

LEFT: The library at Castle Drogo is dominated by a massive granite fireplace in a simplified, almost abstract Gothic style. The forthright expression of undecorated stone and timber in the interior of the building powerfully reinforces the rugged aesthetic.

ation and the hero of *The Thirty-Nine Steps*, summarized the romantic country house aroma as a combination of 'dog and woodsmoke', 'tobacco, the old walls, and wafts of the country coming in at the windows'. Lutyens's son, Robert, echoes the same sentiments in an unpublished memoir:

> It was something special to every building my father had a hand in: if I woke up tomorrow in an unfamiliar room I would know at once, by a scent too subtle to analyse, if I was in one of his houses. It was composed in part of hewn oak and fresh plaster, stone and wood smoke; but it was more than the sum of these, and I have never achieved it in any building of my own.

Lutyens, who never had a country house of his own – the idea of creating a 'little white house' in the country for his wife and family was postponed time and again and never built – spent his life making other people's dreams of living come true. His work, particularly with reference to interior design and furnishing, distilled many contemporary themes: the robust, vernacular honesty of the Arts and Crafts movement, the domestic order and tranquillity beloved by his Edwardian clients and the stately classical tradition handed down from Wren. But in such designs Lutyens achieved something more original than a skilful interweaving of these elements, he also expressed his own very definite tastes.

Decoration, unlike architecture, is ephemeral. Once an architect hands over a building to its occupants – and no handing over was more poignant than

Lutyens's mute relinquishing of Viceroy's House – the owners are naturally free to do as they please with it. Once a house is sold on or the decoration becomes worn and requires replacement, even more changes are inevitable. Less than a decade after her father's death, Lutyens's daughter, Ursula, embarked on an unofficial tour of some of his houses and found many sad alterations, including, horror of horrors, pink bathroom suites. Only a very small number of Lutyens houses today preserve anything approaching the spirit of their original interiors. As the photographic record of Lutyens's early work, compiled by *Country Life*, is in black and white, it can be difficult to gain an appreciation of what these interiors would have looked like in their full textural and material subtleties. Fortunately, Lutyens's letters and the recollections of his daughter Mary help to give some indication of his decorative and design taste, at least in the context of his own houses, a taste shaped to a great degree by his upbringing.

Lutyens's father's lack of commissions and encroaching blindness, the eccentricities he consequently practised in the spirit of economy and the large number of children to feed, clothe and educate meant that the family home, far from being a haven of security, was tumultuous with disarray and became increasingly bohemian as time went on. This disorder in Lutyens's early life had revolted him as much as the

LEFT: No detail was too small for Lutyens, as this intricately designed door furniture from Marshcourt demonstrates.

penury and for the rest of his life he remained as opposed to domestic clutter and muddle as he was terrified of sinking into poverty. The orderly, well-run household was a persistent Edwardian ideal of domesticity, but it chimed perfectly with Lutyens's own deep-seated instincts for simplicity. Perhaps it was because he himself lacked an entirely happy childhood home, and later lacked a settled family life of his own, that he was able to instil the houses he designed for other people with such peace and tranquillity.

The interiors of Lutyens's houses bear witness to his attention to detail. As with all great designers, his imagination could be fired by such apparently insignificant features as door latches and hinges, cupboards, fixtures and fittings. This thorough working out of his design intentions naturally helps to give his houses both a unity and the special, indefinable quality that is his design signature. In the work of many architects who take equivalent pains over details, such obsessional interest can become monotonous and over-bearing. In the case of Lutyens, however, the level of attention is never oppressive, but symptomatic of an irrepressible playfulness and delight. In the small matters of design, as

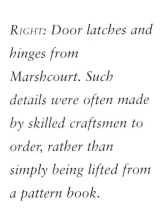

RIGHT: Door latches and hinges from Marshcourt. Such details were often made by skilled craftsmen to order, rather than simply being lifted from a pattern book.

much as the large ones, his aim was always to charm and entrance through the elevating sensation of architectural beauty.

THE EDWARDIAN INTERIOR

Given his taste for simplicity, Lutyens was fortunate to be working at a time that saw a considerable lightening and brightening of the interior. Clutter had reached its apogee in the 1880s, with the High Victorian mélange of curios displayed on every conceivable surface, heavily fringed and tasselled hangings shading rooms already dimly lit and painted in som-

ABOVE: Well-designed door handles and window latches provide daily pleasure on a barely perceptible level – a tactility that Lutyens always took pains to provide.

bre colours, and such a density of furniture that routes were difficult to discern, let alone negotiate. An equal and opposite reaction was not long in coming.

The Arts and Crafts approach to interior design and decoration was to throw out all but the most sympathetic of decorative embellishment and concentrate instead on allowing materials – wood, whitewashed plaster and brick – to express themselves. This radical simplicity, which extended to a preference for plain, traditional country furniture such as might be discovered in an old farmhouse, was often preferred by those who moved in progressive, intellectual or artistic circles. Bernard Shaw recalled a visit to William Morris's London house in Hammersmith and the shock of seeing a bare, unadorned dining table with no concealing tablecloth – an innovation which was considered practically improper at the time. Lutyens, in his early houses, was presenting a version of the same aesthetic, for a clientele whose notion of progressive taste was a fondness for the 'honest country style' of the 'good old days'.

Around the turn of the century, in the strange northern flowering of Art Nouveau, drastically simplified interiors featured a prevalent use of white on walls and furnishings, characterized by the work of Charles Rennie Mackintosh and the Glasgow School. Lutyens was ill at ease with the new art, yet seeing first hand 'white rooms with black furniture, black rooms with white furniture' in Glasgow must have influenced him somewhat, as both white and black became prominent features of his decorative schemes. Perhaps Lutyens could sense that the Glasgow School's poetic but pure decor would serve as a precursor to the severity of modernism, a functional simplicity for which he never felt the slightest sympathy.

By the Edwardian era, it was not just the avant-garde or those with progressive taste who had begun to feel the need for lighter, brighter surroundings. Late Victorian household manuals stressed the need for hygenic domestic conditions: down came the fusty, light-blocking window drapery, out went tester beds with the hangings that so often provided a home for bugs and vermin, up came the layers of carpet to reveal the bare boards beneath. This clean sweep, bringing sunlight and fresh air into the interior, coincided with the first appearance of electricity. Even with their dim wattages, early electrical bulbs were more revealing of dirt and dust than the old gas and oil lights had been; more to the point, electrical bulbs did not discolour walls and ceilings the way gas jets and oil lamps had done. Rooms painted in lighter colours stood a better chance of remaining in such a condition for longer.

For a graphic illustration of this lightening effect on interior decoration, it is worth comparing contemporary photographs taken of the White Drawing Room at Knebworth House before and after it was redecorated around the turn of the century. Knebworth, the ancestral seat of the Lytton family, had passed to Emily's eldest brother, Victor, on the death of their father, Lord Lytton. Lutyens had built Homewood, a small dower house in the grounds, for Emily's mother, and got on well with Victor Lytton's wife, Pamela. Together they planned and carried out extensive redecoration and renovation of both Knebworth House and its garden. In the garden, which was their first joint endeavour, Lutyens brought his characteristic clarity to bear, removing Victorian garden ornaments, clearing away overgrown shrubberies, planting a lime walk and creating a large square pool in the front of the house to reflect the grandeur of the elevation.

ABOVE: The White Drawing Room at Knebworth before redecoration. Lutyens assisted his sister-in-law in transforming both the house and garden.

Changes were no less radical inside. Dark panelling was 'pickled' or limed to a soft pale grey, heavily patterned carpets, swirling with the intricate motifs of High Victoriana, were replaced by carpets in solid pale colours. Silks and light, pretty chintzes were substituted for heavy velvet and brocade. Before redecoration, it is extremely difficult to see why the White Drawing Room should have merited its name. A pale marble surround to the fireplace and a light, although busily patterned plasterwork ceiling provided the only relief in a dark moody room oppressively teeming with ornamentation and

ABOVE: After redecoration, the White Drawing Room was a perfect expression of the Edwardian notion of 'sweetness and light'.

detail. After Lutyens and Lady Lytton had been at work, the difference was dramatic. Delicate crystal chandeliers hung from the plain white ceiling; the newly lightened panelling and pale carpet provided the perfect foil to paintings and an edited collection of decorative objects. Chintz covers to sofas and armchairs introduced a feeling of comfort and well-being. Lutyens, who performed a number of other similar transformations for clients who owned old houses, perfectly captured the 'sweetness and light' that was the essential hallmark of the Edwardian country house style.

One man who played a critical role in the evolution of early twentieth-century taste was Edward Hudson, whose family owned a printing works. Hudson shared the same romantic view of the country as Lutyens's other prosperous upper-middle-class clients and in 1897 had founded *Country Life*. The well-to-do businessmen and their families who formed the principal readership of the new magazine could gaze week after week on lovingly photographed country houses and gardens and dream of building or buying their own. *Country Life,* as a record both of traditional houses and new houses built in the same spirit, served as the first 'lifestyle' magazine, promoting an entire ethos of gracious living based on the virtues of domesticity and proximity to nature. Hudson regularly featured the

LEFT: *Barbie, Lutyens's eldest child, in the kitchen at Lindisfarne, playing with models her father had brought back from a Baltic cruise (1906). Her pose recalls the quiet domesticity of Vermeer paintings.*

BELOW: *Lutyens-designed ladderback dining chairs and sideboard at Deanery Garden.*

houses of his favourite architect, Lutyens, in his magazine. The photography was often by Charles Latham. Shot from a low vantage point, these pictures tend to make the houses look bigger than they actually were.

Hudson was a bachelor and, although shy, liked to entertain. His houses, Deanery Garden and Lindisfarne, were less places to settle down than precisely staged backgrounds, composed with the same degree of care as the photographs in his magazine. This attitude may explain why Hudson found it so easy to part with that 'perfect architectural sonnet', Deanery Garden, only a few years after the house was completed. Lindisfarne, which became his holiday home, was the setting for a series of evocative portraits of Lutyens's children photographed in the austere surroundings of the castle by Charles Latham. Barbara (Barbie) Lutyens, standing by an open casement in the kitchen or peering down a stairwell, is posed in the quiet and contemplative manner of a Vermeer subject. Both Lutyens and Hudson loved seventeenth-century Dutch interiors for their peaceful, homely qualities.

Country Life, for its founder as well as its readers, represented both wish-fulfilment and idealization. Today, when hundreds of glossy publications cater to the interests and aspirations of a more visually sophisticated market, it is difficult to appreciate just how significantly the magazine crystallized the romantic yearnings of the Edwardian era. Looking back, these tranquil Edwardian interiors, poised on the cusp of momentous upheavals that few could have foreseen, are imbued with nostalgia. But in their self-conscious expression of the country living ideal, that nostalgia was already inbuilt.

ARCHITECTURAL COLOUR

'The colour of buildings has both a chromatic and a sculptural sense,' said Lutyens.

Lutyens used colour architecturally. He used it to complement the spatial effects he achieved in his architecture, and he used it as a natural expression of the materials of which his houses were constructed.

In his early picturesque houses, Lutyens's restrained use of colour was almost entirely derived from the palette of his building materials: the soft terracotta of brick and tile and the velvety grey of oak beams set off with pristine whitewashed walls. Ruskin had told Miss Jekyll, when she was planning Munstead Wood, that 'good whitewashed timber and tapestry are the proper walls of rooms in cold climates'. One later visitor to the house, Mary Watts, wrote admiringly in her diary: '... *new* grey tinder-coloured oak beams are my *envy*. Mr Lutyens explains that it is "English" oak. That is nonsense. "Wash it with lime and leave it lying about" that might explain it better. I wonder whether it [will] keep that *velvety grey?*' Limed or 'pickled' oak, bleached to a pale neutrality, had its own quiet dignity; equally important, while not precisely distressed, the lightened timber did suggest the weathering effect of time.

RIGHT: The West Bedroom at Lindisfarne is furnished with a Flemish seventeenth-century carved and panelled oak bed. The room had formerly been used as a gunpowder magazine when the castle was a fort.

LEFT: *A pair of Lutyens's Napoleon chairs flank the fireplace in the London drawing room of Candia Lutyens and Paul Peterson. The sofa was made to an original Lutyens design of 1929. The yellow colour scheme emphasizes the warmth of the south-facing aspect.*

The use of white as a principal colour for walls was refreshing and new at the end of the nineteenth century. William Morris had been a pioneer in this respect and many of the walls at his Red House, designed by Philip Webb, were whitewashed. Morris had very decided views on the integrity of the finish: '... honest whitewash ... on which sun and shadow play so pleasantly.' Clouds, the country house of the Wyndham family, also designed by Webb, was famous – or notorious – for its use of plain white walls to set off the patterns of Morris fabrics. Webb remarked to his client, 'When you decide on doing any whitewashing as advised by William Morris, let me know; there is a way of doing even this properly.' Unfortunately, what Morris considered the proper whitewashing method to be has not been recorded.

White, for the Victorians, was the shock of the new. But, in a sense, it was worse than that. 'Honest' whitewash was the serviceable treatment for utilitarian areas of the house; it was what one might expect to find painted on the walls 'below stairs', in a maid's bedroom or a privy. The notion that white could be the background for reception rooms in a fine house was radical in the extreme.

By the time Lutyens came to design his picturesque houses in the Surrey countryside, the Arts and Crafts aesthetic had taken greater hold of the public imagination. Whitewash was simply seen as an appropriately country finish, unpretentious and homely in its associations. Its inherent domesticity, and the yearly renewal necessary to keep the finish pristine, spoke of good housekeeping, as the opening passage of *The Wind in the Willows*, published in 1908, reveals:

The Mole had been working very hard all morning, spring-cleaning his little home. First with brooms, then with dusters; then on ladders and steps and chairs, with a brush and a pail of whitewash; till he had dust in his throat and eyes, and splashes of whitewash all over his black fur, and an aching back and weary arms.

White thus had the Edwardian seal of approval; it was possible even to admire it. When Betty Balfour (Emily's eldest sister) and her husband acquired one of Lutyens's early Surrey houses, Fisher's Hill near Woking, Emily's brother noted, 'The whitewash in the kitchen is one of the most lovely wall surfaces I ever saw.'

The whitewash of Lutyens's day was very different from our white emulsion. Before chemical paint formulations were introduced after the Second World War, whitewash might have been either limewash or distemper, both of which created a subtle chalky finish of some depth and character. Neither would have contained bluing agents, which give most modern white paints a hard, 'whiter than white' brilliance. Lutyens set off the chalky white used for masonry and plaster with a pure, pristine white on wood-

RIGHT: *Lutyens enjoyed strong colour. In the dining room at Lindisfarne, the walls are painted a vibrant Prussian blue. The brick floor is laid in a herringbone pattern, one of Lutyens's favourites.*

LEFT: Black, according to Lutyens, is 'conducive to magnificence'. He believed that in low northrn light black was essential to give life to white mouldings and plasterwork. The black walls of the library in Candia Lutyens's and Paul Peterson's London house provide the perfect foil to the crisp white ceiling with its decorative mouldings. Used in layers of glazes, rather than an even flat tone, black can be particularly rich, glowing with all the reflected colours in a room.

work and doors, a treatment which accentuated the crispness of wooden mouldings.

Lutyens also used white as a foil for colour and activity in the interior: the ballroom at Viceroy's House is a case in point. The lower portion of the walls were clad in white marble, the upper portions were left plain. Mirrors hung on the walls and crystal chandeliers were suspended from the ceiling. The idea of this white sparkling background was to intensify the effect of dancers in their brightly coloured clothes. Unfortunately, the walls were later painted.

Lutyens was not particularly innovative in his use of white, but he caused more of a stir with his preference for black as the main background colour for large reception rooms. 'Black is an important factor in all decoration,' said Lutyens in an address to the Architectural Association, 'I often wonder why black is not more frequently used. If you want great dignity in decoration, use black. It is conducive to magnificence.'

If black was not much used in Lutyens's day, it is even more of a rarity in decoration today. Superficially, black rooms sound particularly grim, especially in a climate where natural light levels can be low. Black, far from being 'conducive to magnificence' might well be considered a little too Gothic for words. Yet, Lutyens's black rooms were not all black, nor was the black a flat, absorbing tone that sucked the light and life from rooms. On the contrary, as Mary Lutyens recalled: 'There was nothing dead about this; indeed the glossy black background reflected all the colours in the room.' The black was painted over a complex layering of undercoat so that it glowed. In all three of Lutyens's family homes, the front drawing room was painted black in a semi-gloss finish, graphically contrasted with a white ceiling and white woodwork. Homewood, the house Lutyens designed for his mother-in-law, had a black hall set off by white woodwork. The lightening contrast of the white was an important factor in the success of this striking decorative scheme, and so was the finish.

Wherever possible, Lutyens avoided applied decoration. Different colours signalled different surfaces; often materials themselves were used to provide graphic colour contrast. The hall and staircase at Gledstone, in North Yorkshire, demonstrated a particularly powerful example of this black and white theme in the context of a classical design. Against the austerity of pure white, black skirting, picture rail and dado defined the proportional relationships. The staircase had alternating black and white marble treads and a black coved ceiling.

But Lutyens's decorative schemes were not exclusively monochromatic. Strong, brilliant colour was also used on walls and floors. The dining room at Bloomsbury Square was painted red (rose-madder mixed with black, according to Mary Lutyens), while the nursery was decorated in the powerful complementary combination of blue and yellow. The small hall was papered in silver and had vermilion skirtings. The silver was not highly reflective, but had, in Mary Lutyens's recollection, more the quality of 'that lead coloured lining to antique tea caddies'. The wooden drawing room floor was painted green, dragged over three undercoats of white. An emerald green floor, highly varnished, was also a feature of

the drawing room at Bedford Square, which, like its predecessor, had black walls and white woodwork – together with yellow curtains. The green served as a foil to the rich reds of Persian rugs.

Green was evidently a favourite colour. Lutyens used a particular shade of greeny-blue tile in two bathrooms at Marshcourt; green tiling was also a feature of his early fireplaces in the vernacular style. He was very fond of green marble. Oak boards at Lambay and Lindisfarne were painted greenish duck-egg blue; Lutyens habitually wore shirts of the same colour. Heathcote's black marble stair was enlivened by a carpet of strong green, while the columns in the hall were green Siberian marble.

Also at Heathcote, Lawrence Weaver mentions a suite of Lutyens-designed furniture painted 'the cloudy blue which Mr Lutyens so likes to use'; the entrance vestibule ceiling was painted 'an indefinite blue' and in one of the bedrooms, a fireplace grate was 'set in a sea of blue which suggests no name'. These cool, distant blues seem to feature more strongly in Lutyens's classical interiors, where they would have perfectly complemented crisp white mouldings and creamy stonework.

There was nothing faint-hearted about Lutyens's colour schemes. The pairings of complementaries – blue and yellow, red and green – gave added punch. At Folly Farm, originally a small Berkshire cottage

RIGHT: *Another striking use of black occurred in Lutyens's original decorative scheme for Folly Farm, where black walls were offset by the vibrant accent of balconies lacquered red.*

LEFT: Green was one of Lutyens's favourite interior colours, particularly for tilework. The small handmade tiles that line this bathroom at Marshcourt unite the surfaces in a regular grid. Handmade tiles display a certain irregularity of glazing which adds vitality.

which Lutyens enlarged first in 1904 and then substantially in 1912, the double-height hall was painted black, with white architectural detail. Balconies at the upper level, overlooking the hall from either end, had Chippendale-style fretwork lacquered scarlet (the balconies are now gone).

Floors, as well as walls and detail, offered Lutyens the opportunity to use colour 'architecturally'. Lutyens's floors are almost a study in themselves, from the harmonious use of brick and timber in his earlier buildings to set pieces in marble in his later classical works. In this classical mode, contrasting materials or colours were employed to create striking geometric patterns which emphasized routes through space or provided a floor-level focus of interest. Stylized star shapes were a familiar motif for these grand exercises in marble; several Lutyens patterns have in recent years been reproduced in linoleum by a leading manufacturer. But it is the Durbar Hall at Viceroy's House which displays one of Lutyens' most extravagant floors. Made of highly polished contrasting black and white stone, its pattern of circles and broad connecting lines is huge in scale. Christopher Hussey quotes a contemporary observer, Robert Byron, who wrote: 'The pattern of the floor alone is so huge as to leave the entrant breathless, almost frightened to make his first two or three steps. In its glacial porphyry surface the jasper

LEFT: Lutyens often used colour 'architecturally', as it arose in different materials, rather than as applied decoration. The staircase at Gledstone Hall, with its black and white marble steps, is a case in point.

reflections of the encircling columns are intersected by broad white bands and curves edged in black, two of which lead, direct as an arterial road, from the entrance to the thrones.'

ARCHITECTURAL DETAIL

All of Lutyens's work is rich in what, for the want of a better term, one might call 'architectural detail'. Furthermore, the detailing is exceptionally varied, spanning centuries of architectural style, yet often betraying the architect's characteristic signature at the same time. Detail, particularly in its contemporary sense, tends to imply something superfluous or additional to the principal design. The recent vogue for recreating period styles has encouraged this perception, by focusing on elements such as cornices, mantelpieces, picture and dado rails, which can be applied to a room to create the desired historical effect. With Lutyens, however, detailing was not the decorative icing on the cake; it was part of the cake. Lutyens often adopted an arrangement whereby rounded archways flanked a fireplace. Superficially, this might seem a classical embellishment, but the deeper purpose was to enhance the sense of space. None of Lutyens's details was ever incidental. His great familiarity with the entire architectural vocabulary also meant that he was able to manipulate the design of such details with masterful ease.

No one designed staircases, halls or doorways better than Lutyens. The drama and theatre of movement through a space, of changing levels, of arrival, constantly intrigued him. Aside from such spatial experiences, the detailing of such features in

LEFT: Looking down the staircase at 24 Cheyne Walk, London, a house that Lutyens designed for Cecil Baring (Lord Revelstoke) but which has since been demolished. One of the treads of the stair met the entablature of a ground floor doorway, an elegant and complex architectural solution.

RIGHT: Spiral staircase at Midland Bank, Poultry. The spiral, a natural pattern occurring in shells, plant forms and galaxies, conforms to ratios based on the Fibonacci progression. Consciously or not, Lutyens often used such ratios in his work.

either vernacular or classical idiom provided endless scope for virtuosity.

His early staircases, typically made of timber, had low, broad treads, which gave a measured, dignified pace. At Marshcourt, the detailing of the main staircase betrays Lutyens's love of wood as a material. Each stair is a single piece of carved timber, rather than being pieced from a separate riser and tread. Pegged joints stud the surface of the stair, providing a rhythmic expression of constructional integrity, which is nevertheless more about poetry than strict honesty in the Arts and Crafts sense. The

LEFT: Marble staircase at Britannic House, London, one of Lutyens's few large commercial commissions. The chair, made to an original Lutyens design of 1925 by Lutyens Design Associates, is one of many items of furniture he created for Viceroy's House, New Delhi and was intended for 'Her Excellency's Sitting Room'.

newel posts are all different, carved into familiar English classical shapes. One features a squirrel with a tail shaped like an acanthus leaf: the model for the carving was originally made in plaster by Lady Chance, Lutyens's sculptor-client who lived at Orchards.

In his later classical mode, Lutyens grew to prefer marble for his staircases. At Heathcote, as previously mentioned, he persuaded his client to have a black marble staircase instead of one made from oak – the 'persuasion' more accurately taking the form of going ahead and doing what he felt to be right.

One of his most masterful exercises in the detailing of a stair unfortunately no longer exists. In 1930 Lutyens designed a London house for Cecil Baring, the owner of Lambay Castle, who was now Lord Revelstoke. The house, at Cheyne Walk in Chelsea, was pulled down several years after completion and all that now remains are contemporary photographs. Nevertheless, the spiral stair at Cheyne Walk provides one of the most striking examples of Lutyens's ability to think in three dimensions. Christopher Hussey describes the effect:

> A spiral, the underside of one of its treads coincided with the entablature of a doorway beneath it – itself identical with the other ground-floor doorways. The apparently fortuitous effect was a perfect instance of Lutyens' lightly worn skill, for the achievement of the 'coincidence' dictated the staircase's width, angle of ascent, and the number of treads, and in its turn was controlled by the height of the lower storey.

The amazing complexity of the design, linking two of Lutyens's favourite features, stair and door, resulted in a great sense of ease and inevitability.

At Homewood, the dower house at Knebworth, there is another example of Lutyens achieving a striking unity of stair and entrance. The staircase, set between two internal doorways, is framed by its own entrance, an open archway the width of the stair. With the short flights of stairs rising up beyond the arch that obscures their ultimate destination, the arrangement provokes a tantalizing sense of discovery that leads the eye onwards.

Fireplaces were another focus of interest. 'A good fireplace is essential in all rooms,' said Lutyens. He was so fond of the mantelpieces at Bloomsbury Square that he took them with him to Bedford Square, a small comfort for a wrenching move. His persistent delight in fireplace design can be adduced from the fact that nearly every fireplace in Viceroy's House is different. Fireplaces, for Lutyens, were of psychological as well as architectural importance: their warmth, light and communality forming the core of the house.

Unlike staircases, which were generally designed to follow suit with the main architectural theme, whether vernacular or classical, a contrasting style was often adopted for the fire surround, particularly in the early houses. When designing in the picturesque fashion, Lutyens often suggested the passage of time in his newly built houses by combining different historical styles in the architectural detailing. A classical or Wren-influenced fireplace was one way to suggest a later modification of an old building,

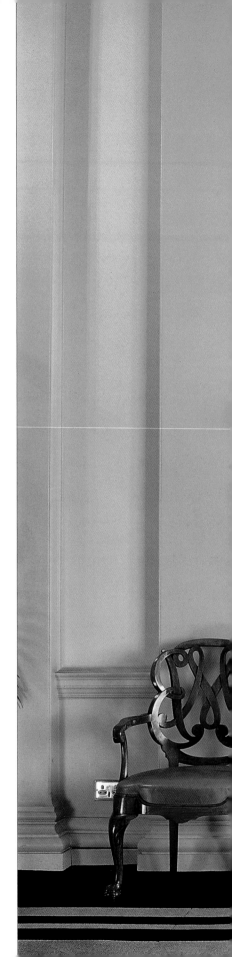

*R*IGHT: *Interior of Midland Bank, Poultry, showing a Lutyens fireplace in a restrained classical mode. Lutyens evidently gained much pleasure from the design of such features – nearly every fireplace at Viceroy's House, for example, is of different design.*

LEFT: Another fireplace at Midland Bank, Poultry. The bold detailing of the white marble surround provides an effective contrast to the wood panelled walls, with their delicate carved flourishes.

but it also introduced a leavening element of surprise and contrast.

At Munstead Wood the massive fireplace in the sitting room has an overhanging hood in the Arts and Crafts medieval manner. But already at Orchards, which followed soon after, the fireplace in Lady Chance's studio was a huge classical affair that took up most of one wall.

Little Thakeham, set deep in the Sussex countryside, was, in Lutyens's own estimation, 'the best of the bunch' of his private houses. In the main hall the classical interior detailing provides a striking contrast to the romantic exterior. The wide stone fireplace, with its strongly expressed bolection mouldings, and lining of tiles set on edge, punctuates the stonework that partially clads the room. Elsewhere in the house, the wide brick-lined fireplace in the parlour reverts to a medieval theme, while the library's marble fireplace has the same classical mouldings, in the manner of Wren, as the fireplace in the hall. In a typical Lutyens touch, the two upright oak panels that frame the fireplace open to reveal cupboards.

One of Lutyens's most famous fireplaces, however, has an almost abstract sculptural power that sets it apart from historical style. The granite fireplace in the library at Castle Drogo is almost proto-modern in its minimal detailing and massive expression of material.

Classical insertions into what at first glance appear traditional or vernacular houses also took the form of decorative plasterwork, panelling and pilasters. At Marshcourt, superficially a Tudor house, the interiors were almost completely classical

LEFT: The virtuosity of such detailing as this marble column and its ornate Corinthian capital reveals Lutyens's deep understanding of classical elements and the breadth of his architectural vocabulary.

RIGHT AND BELOW RIGHT: Marshcourt is set on a hill overlooking the River Test, in an area of England that is still predominantly rural. The carved chalk frieze in the hall at Marshcourt – a superb example of craftsmanship – depicts the local wildflowers of the district arranged in classical swags and clusters. The decorative tour de force *also provides an important textural contrast, inset in oak panelling and beneath a plasterwork ceiling.*

in their detailing. The drawing room ceiling features particularly elaborate plasterwork in high relief, with lizards sunning themselves on branching boughs of fruit and flowers. The dining room, on the other side of the hall from the drawing room, is entirely lined in quartered panels of walnut veneer, a treatment where detail meets wall finish meets furniture. In the hall itself, decorative detail provides the opportunity to play with contrasting textures and materials. At either end of the hall, two friezes executed in chalk set into the oak panelling portray, in classically swagged fashion, the wild flowers of the locality, a witty marriage of the formal and classical, and the naturalistic.

FURNITURE AND FITTINGS

From the earliest days of his engagement, Lutyens expressed very decided views about the type of furnishings he preferred. It is just as well that his wife-to-be, Lady Emily, had little experience of housekeeping and no particular aesthetic bent of her own, otherwise the potential for domestic conflict could have been vastly multiplied. In the letters Lutyens wrote to Emily during their courtship, he indicated – and illustrated – just how he proposed to furnish their first home together. The memoir which Mary Lutyens wrote about her parents' marriage lists some of Lutyens's particular antipathies.

Father never lost certain prejudices – against loose covers, for instance, silk lampshades, fringes on anything, fitted or pile carpets, flowers indoors, fish knives, glasses with stems, and vacuum clean-

RIGHT: The dining room at Marshcourt is a superb example of a fitted room. Entirely lined in quartered panels of walnut veneer, which contrasts with the pristine white plasterwork and ornate ceiling mouldings, the beautifully detailed and crafted room displays all of Lutyens's love of materials, fine workmanship and geometry. Lutyens developed a series of rules of angles and proportions that he applied throughout his work – rules which give both buildings and details a very characteristic quality.

ABOVE: *An imposing pedimented doorway at Midland Bank, Poultry, enriched by carved swags. The integral clock is a typical Lutyens touch.*

RIGHT: *Detail from the hall at Marshcourt, showing the rich combination of materials, finely worked: oak panelling, marble pilasters and plasterwork cornice.*

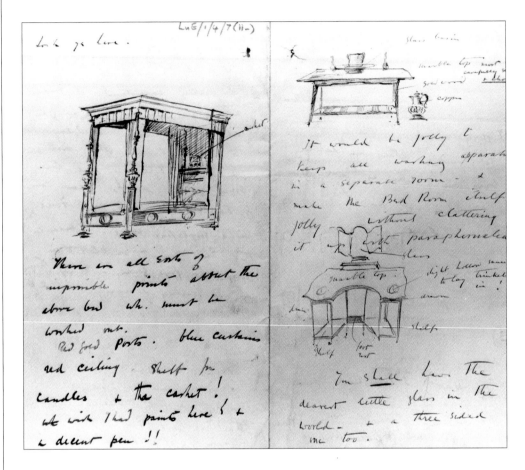

LEFT: An extract from one of Lutyens's letters to his wife-to-be, Lady Emily, showing his sketch for a bed and other bedroom furniture.

RIGHT: The Italianate bed that Lutyens proposed in his letter, with its high headboard and polished steel posts, was made exactly to his specifications in light oak (1897).

ers which he said ruined any carpet. Where we did have carpets, as on the front stairs (the back stairs were left to their cold stone), the landings and Mother's bedroom, they were always the same, designed by him – dark grey hair-cord with a narrow yellow and black border. Our glasses were also designed by him – of a tumbler type in three diffferent sizes, for water, wine and port … I believe that some of Father's prejudices were dictated by economy; black horsehair never wore out and never had to be cleaned; it could be sponged when dirty; stemless glasses seldom broke; card lampshades were cheaper than silk.

Mary Lutyens goes on to ascribe her father's aversion to cut flowers to an occasion when he mistakenly picked a flower in Miss Jekyll's garden which was intended for seed and was reprimanded.

It was not the case that all Lutyens's prejudices arose from an instinct for economy. His preference for close-covered furniture, for instance, seems to have been the result of the slip-shod nature of his childhood home, where clutter and family detritus was shoved out of the way under the flounces of loose covers when company was expected. Black horsehair, aside from being hardwearing and dirt-disguising, is also a very graphic way of revealing

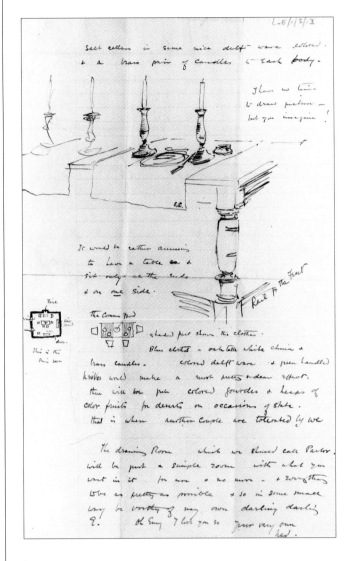

the clean-lined contours of upholstered furniture.

Lutyens, with his Arts and Crafts upbringing, had a particular fondness for simplicity in design and hatred of meaningless elaboration. A wedding present that came in for some pointed invective was a silver and cut-glass inkstand. The stand was fashioned out of an old wine coaster, just the sort of masquerade that Lutyens hated. Hussey quotes Lutyens's reaction: 'Why do people always turn something into something else then stroke their tum-

ABOVE: Lutyens imagined his future domestic arrangements in some detail, down to place settings. His dining table was to be set with individual blue linen mats draped across the width of the table, each with its own pair of brass candlesticks.

RIGHT: Lutyens's refectory-style oak dining table, as proposed in his letter to Lady Emily, reveals a Dutch influence.

mies and call themselves of good taste!' Neither was he pleased to receive a toast rack.

Lutyens's detailed plans for his first married home – 'I am most exercised about Towels' – show a taste for elegant simplicity, verging on austerity, coupled with a countervailing instinct for richness. What is particularly interesting about these plans is that they reveal, at a very early date, elements that would be present in a more developed form in his later designs for furniture and fittings.

He was keen to keep the bedroom free from clutter. It was to be painted white, with 'gay flowery curtains'. He sketched out an Italianate tester bed, with a high headboard and imagined placing a cassone or chest at its foot. The bed, subsequently made to his specifications, was in light oak with polished steel posts. Accompanying pieces, specially made for Bloomsbury Square, later included a dressing table for Emily with a three-leaf mirror, a refectory table for the dining room and a linen press, all made of light oak.

That still quality of a Vermeer interior Lutyens so admired comes across in his ideas for table setting. The light oak table was not to be covered with 'a great sheet of superfine damask' but individually set with light blue linen table mats draped at intervals across the width to reveal the natural finish. Each place setting was to have its own pair of brass candlesticks and Delft salt cellar. Knives would be green-handled, the china white Wedgwood: 'Blue cloths, oak table, white china, and brass candles, coloured delft ware and green-handled knives would make a most pretty and dear effect.' He added that on special occasions, heaps of coloured fruit would add a touch of festivity. This fully imagined scene, composed with a painterly regard for colour and complementary textures, reveals Lutyens's uncanny ability to animate interiors, to project a way of living into his designs. He had not yet found Bloomsbury Square when he was busily planning these arrangements, but they eventually materialized exactly as he wished. The simplicity of the table was to be matched by a simplicity of fare: 'Food matters not! except how it is served …' This did not prevent him from imagining the progress of a typical day of married bliss, with meals described in some detail.

If Lutyens's taste inclined after those poised seventeenth-century Dutch interiors, the only paintings he wished to hang on his own walls were pictures that were 'small, Italian in feeling, gorgeous in colour, and in exquisite frames'. Later, Carpaccio's paintings of St Ursula provided inspiration when he came to design beds for his daughters, Barbara and Ursula. Made of bergère wickerwork framed by mahogany, a favourite combination, they were always known as the 'St Ursula beds'.

Emily provided no opposition to Lutyens's plans and had few suggestions of her own to make. 'Ned likes nothing that is not simple,' she wrote. 'He says the most beautiful things are always the simplest.' Like many architects, Lutyens was rather more at a loss when it came to conjuring up the furnishings of the drawing room. He had declared to his wife-to-be that comfort was not a priority as far as he was concerned and, indeed, despite the 'armchairs and sofas etc' which he envisaged, the planned writing table and low bookcases seem to indicate he could better imagine working than relaxing. The drawing room would also include the red lacquer cabinet that Lutyens had bought for Emily early on in their courtship, as an oblique announcement of the seriousness of his intentions. For quite some time, the drawing room remained unfurnished except for that cabinet, a Chinese screen and a pair of Delft horses, which were wedding presents. The lack of furnishing was perhaps prophetic; instead of spending quiet conjugal evenings at his own drawing room fireside, he generally spent most evenings working. In his memoir, Robert Lutyens explores the contradictory nature of his father's taste:

I fell to pondering on the strange manner in which my father's Victorian boyhood and the influences of his youth had combined to form his taste – the taste of an artist superimposed on the temperament of a puritan; how he had sought to realize in his surroundings the material symbols of a social creed he was not consciously aware of: the oak board and blue linen cloth; the pewterware; the well-stocked still room and all housewifely thrift and duty; and how Renaissance craftsmanship had later aroused his wonder and admiration, and inspired his own virtuosity, but had never shaken his distaste for the parade of opulence for any manifestation of emotion bordering on vulgarity. He adored refinement as much as he detested luxury.

Lutyens's preference for simplicity had probably been influenced by Gertrude Jekyll, who furnished Munstead Wood in the plain country style. Miss Jekyll, who was an inveterate magpie, collected country furniture. The following passage summarizes the comfortable aesthetic:

The floor was well-worn red brick, and on the wide hearth burnt a fire of logs, between two attractive chimney-corners tucked away in the wall, well out of any suspicion of draught. A couple of high-backed settles, facing each other on either side of the fire, gave further sitting accommodation for the sociably disposed. In the middle of the room stood a long table of plain boards placed on trestles, with benches down each side … Rows of spotless plates winked from the shelves of the dresser at the far end of the room, and from the rafters overhead hung hams, bundles of dried herbs, nets of onions, and baskets of eggs. It seemed a place where heroes could fitly feast after victory, where weary harvesters could line up in scores along the table and keep their Harvest Home with mirth and song, or where two or three friends of simple tastes could sit about as they pleased and eat and smoke and talk in comfort and contentment. The ruddy brick floor smiled up at the smoky ceiling; the oaken settles, shiny with long wear, exchanged cheerful glances with each other; plates on the dresser grinned at pots on the shelf, and the merry firelight flickered and played over everything without distinction.

Written by another romantic Edwardian, Kenneth Grahame, this extract from *The Wind in the Willows* actually describes Badger's kitchen, but the same kitchen and its traditional old English furnishings, could well have been found in Lutyens's early vernacular houses. A contemporary photograph of the dining room at Deanery Garden shows simple ladderback dining chairs designed by Lutyens ranged round a carved and scrubbed oak table. The sideboard, also to Lutyens's design, displayed an orderly domestic array of pewter plates and a Delft-patterned dinner service. The kitchen furniture at Castle Drogo, all of which was designed by Lutyens, is in plain scrubbed oak and includes a massive circular worktable placed directly under the central rotunda which top lights the space. At the same time, what Lutyens's clients also wanted was something with more of the grandeur of Toad Hall, 'a handsome, dignified old house of mellowed red brick' with a banqueting hall. Furnishing grand rooms very simply, contrasting the humble with the sophisticated,

was one way in which Lutyens satisfied both apparently contradictory aspirations.

Within the context of this early crafted aesthetic, Lutyens gave his buildings immense tactility by paying attention to details which less thorough-minded designers might simply have lifted from a pattern book. Gertrude Jekyll described the effect in *Home and Garden:*

> Internal fittings that are constantly seen and handled, such as window-fastenings, hinges, bolts and door-latches, are specially designed and specially made, so that they are in perfect proportion, for size, weight, and strength, to the wood and iron-work to which they are related. There are no random choosings from the iron-monger's pattern-book, no clashing of styles, no meretricious ornamentation, no impudence of cast-iron substitute for honest hand-work, no moral slothfulness in the providing of all these lesser finishings. It takes more time, more trouble; it may even take a good deal of time and trouble, but then it is just right, and to see and know that it is right is a daily reward and never-ending source of satisfaction.

Such details, which fit so perfectly into the hand, provided daily, tactile pleasure on an almost subconscious level.

LEFT: How to curtain a casement window, according to Lutyens. This neo-Gothic window in the dining room at Lindisfarne features a hinged rod, so that the entire curtain could be swung free from the window.

Lutyens was an orderly man, who valued neatness highly among the domestic virtues. The service areas of his houses were always beautifully fitted out, particularly appealing in their human scale and the domesticity of their treatment. As an architect for whom 'everyone and everything had a house' he was especially thoughtful in his provision of cupboard space. Lutyens's houses are eminently covetable for their cupboards alone. He instinctively understood the particular housekeeping pleasure of stowing things away in their appropriate place.

Providing enough cupboards was a particular challenge for a client such as Gertrude Jekyll, who was a considerable accumulator. The beautiful cupboards ranged along the length of the upper gallery at Munstead Wood was an arrangement he repeated at Marshcourt, where the first-floor corridor has a complete run of cupboards for linen, each with their own oak door. At Heathcote, which is entirely classical, the china cupboards on the first floor corridor have exquisite arched glazed doors with a fine teardrop pattern in the glazing bars. Glazed bookshelves set in alcoves to either side of the fireplace in the morning room have drop-flap writing desks. Built in with the architecture and entirely sympathetic in terms of detailing, such practical features demonstrate Lutyens's thorough appreciation of the domestic ideal.

One characteristic Lutyenesque practicality concerned curtains. In his early romantic houses, and in romantic reconstructions such as Lindisfarne, windows were generally of the casement variety, set deep within the wall. The degree of recess meant that there was not enough room for curtains to be pulled to either side of the window without blocking a great deal of light. Lutyens's solution, which he used repeatedly, was to hang the curtains on hinged rods, which could be swung clear of the window and preserve the quality of light.

Lutyens designed a great deal of furniture for his clients, but these pieces were expected to co-exist happily with antiques and furnishings of the client's own possession. He advised Ida Streatfeild, for whom he built Fulbrook, one of his early Surrey houses, to make one-eighth scale plans of her furniture and move them about on the plans of the house to determine ideal arrangement. For Viceroy's House, however, Lutyens designed nearly all of the furniture, a vast undertaking. The Delhi legacy, preserved in sheaves of detailed and annotated drawings, is an invaluable source of Lutyens's designs in his late classical manner.

Furnishing New Delhi came late on in the progress of the work, towards the end of the 1920s. For the previous fifteen years, however, Lutyens had been urging anyone who would listen to set up a school of design and craft in Delhi to train local craftsmen and revive traditional Indian skills. The craft school never materialized. Lutyens had been particularly keen to use traditional Indian cottons, *khuddar*, hand printed from wood blocks, as furnishing materials –

RIGHT: The kitchen at Lindisfarne, with its coal-fired range installed in a wide stone fireplace. Lutyens designed the oak dresser specially for the room, including its handles.

which would have provided another example of humble vernacular elements serving to deflate architectural grandeur. But when the fabrics were ordered, the results proved too crude to be acceptable.

There was more success with the carpets. Specially woven in Kashmir, the carpet designs for the great state rooms at Viceroy's House were taken from sixteenth- and seventeenth-century Persian originals, a period which represented the height of carpet-making artistry and design. Patterns, dyes and materials were faithfully reproduced. The carpets took 500 weavers two years to make.

Lutyens designed not only the furniture for Viceroy's House, including the Viceroy's throne, but also most of the light fittings, and all the fireplaces, down to the fenders, fire-irons and firebacks. A team of Indian cabinet-makers was trained to make the furniture. The principal material used was teak, but other exotic hardwoods, including padouk, blackwood, koko and ebony, were used decoratively.

India, in common with many Eastern societies, has little in the way of a furniture tradition as it is understood in the West. Instead of the innumerable types of seat and cabinet furniture, tables and beds, that have evolved over centuries in Europe and North America, Indian furnishing relies on a few simple multi-purpose forms, such as the *chowki*, a low couch on short legs which serves equally as a base for sleeping, reclining or sitting. More upright furniture is largely redundant in a culture that prefers to sit close to the ground. But jointed wooden furniture is also impractical in a climate where extreme variations of temperature and humidity inevitably cause a great deal of movement as the wood swells and contracts. Many of the English antiques shipped out to New Delhi did not survive for long.

Lutyens was designing furniture for New Delhi at the time when he was increasingly preoccupied by geometric interplay. Like most of his later furniture, these pieces are strongly classical in inspiration, with exquisite refinement of design and detail.

There is nothing showy about Lutyens's furniture; the designs have their own innate integrity. They are also highly architectural and very seldom are there straight lines. With their curved, tapering shapes, Lutyens's pieces often prove fiendishly difficult to make. An occasional table, designed in 1930 for Viceroy's House, reveals a characteristically Lutyenesque play on the relationship between the circle, square and triangle. The base is triangular in structure; the three open sides each comprise a circle within a square. The circular top swivels so that its three leaves fold down to transform the top into a triangle matching the base. This highly complex design is structurally very difficult to achieve. Simpler is a tripod side table, also designed for Viceroy's House, in 1925. The circular top rests on three legs which sweep out into an exaggerated but pleasingly simplified flourish, almost an abstraction of a claw foot.

Lutyens's ingenuity is revealed by his design for an expanding dining table, designed for a private dining room at New Delhi in 1930. The table, designed to seat twelve when closed, was eight feet across, but could be stretched out to sixteen feet in diameter to seat twenty. The support for the extending leaves in the middle takes the form of lazy tongs. When the

ABOVE: Occasional table made by Lutyens Design Associates to an original design of 1930. Many of Lutyens's designs are highly complex and prove extremely difficult to construct.

'tongs' are concertinaed, the legs of the tongs are aligned along the table's diameter out of the way; when the table is opened, the legs are symmetrically arranged so as to provide no obstruction.

Lutyens also designed sofas and armchairs for New Delhi. An armchair and its accompanying stool designed for two of the bedrooms at Viceroy's House rest on moulded wooden bases. The curved lines of the chair back and arms look simple, but

were precisely designed as sections of compass-drawn circles; this purity of geometry contributes to the elegance and rightness of the final effect. In another design for a three-seat sofa and two matching chairs, Lutyens incorporated the 'Delhi Bell' motif in the wooden frieze that supports each piece. The bell motif – a silent bell incapable of ringing – refers to the Indian traditional belief that dynasties fall to the sound of ringing bells. Lutyens used the same motif in many different contexts in New Delhi.

The circle-back chair, designed for bedrooms in New Delhi in 1930, is a geometric *tour de force*. The gently splayed back is an open framework of interlocking circles, which increase in size and thickness from top to bottom. The arms are in the form of two sweeping semicircles. Equally elegant is the spider-back chair, which Lutyens used in several locations, including Campion Hall in Oxford.

Lutyens's own favourite chair, however, was the Napoleon chair. He first had a pair of these chairs made the year he and his family moved to Mansfield Street. As Mary Lutyens remembered:

> We always called it 'the Napoleon chair' because, apparently, it bore a resemblance to a chair in which Napoleon was sitting in some painting which my father said he had once seen. This has

RIGHT: The kitchen in Candia Lutyens's and Paul Peterson's house is fitted and furnished in the Lutyens manner.

BELOW: Original design for the circle-back chair of 1930. The circles become progressively larger from the top and the thickness of the rings becomes wider.

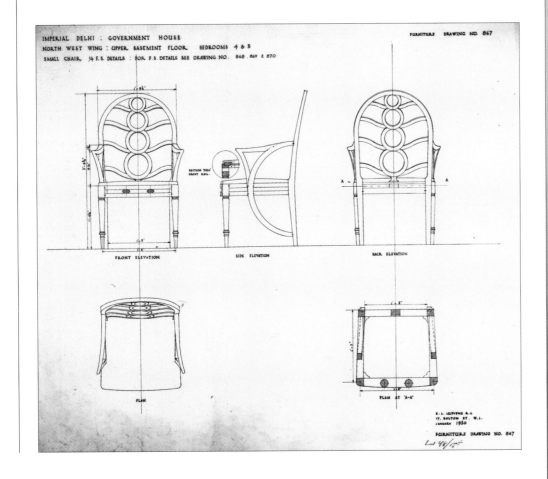

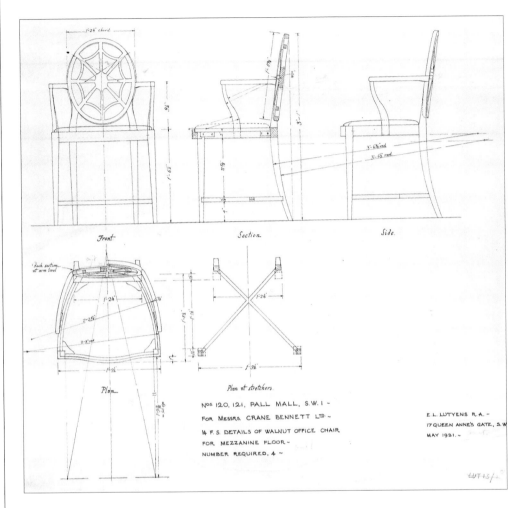

Front

Section.

Side.

Plan

Plan at stretchers.

Nᴼˢ 120, 121, PALL MALL, S.W. 1 ~
FOR MESSRS. CRANE BENNETT LTᴰ. ~
¼ F. S. DETAILS OF WALNUT OFFICE CHAIR
FOR MEZZANINE FLOOR ~
NUMBER REQUIRED, 4 ~

E. L. LUTYENS R.A. ~
17 QUEEN ANNE'S GATE, S.W
MAY 1931. ~

BELOW: The spider-back chair appears in sketches of an imaginary house that Lutyens made for a friend, Captain Day. The sketch shows the Captain's dining saloon.

ABOVE: Drawings of the spider-back chair, dated 1931. The spider-back motif was used by Lutyens for chairs in several of his buildings, and was probably inspired by a similar Hepplewhite design.

since been confirmed by the discovery of an early nineteenth-century drawing of Napoleon in his study at the Tuileries, in which a similar chair appears.

A pair of these chairs stood on either side of the fireplace in our front drawing room. With one leg thrown over the end, my father found it the most comfortable chair he had ever sat in. (Indeed, he loved the chair so much that he had a pair of them made in miniature for the Library of Queen Mary's Dolls' House in 1924.) The black horsehair

RIGHT: Three-seat sofa and matching chairs designed in 1929 for New Delhi, photographed at Britannic House. The 'Delhi Bell' is used as the point of support for each seat.

ABOVE: *This elaborate Lutyens chair, designed for Midland Bank, Poultry, features the entwined initials M B.*

LEFT: *A Lutyens-inspired table setting: glass tumblers, white Wedgwood, green bone-handled knives and blue linen placemats. The watch was Lutyens's own design, made by Cartier and features his design for the family crest – concentric stars in a geometric pattern.*

Another Marshcourt example diffused the light of the bulb with a glass disc held in place with iron clips; above the bulb were decorative beads. A version of the same design was also made for Viceroy's House, New Delhi.

LEFT: *One of a pair of hanging shades designed for Gledstone Hall, this charming design features a glass disc to diffuse the light source, an idea well ahead of its time – a similar solution to the problem of glare can be seen in many contemporary light fittings.*

RIGHT: *One of the clocks Lutyens designed for Viceroy's House. The hands expand like tongs to reach their fullest extent at nine and three. The key is in the form of a pansy – a pun on* pensée, *and thus a reminder to wind the clock!*

BELOW: *Design for a nursery clock in the form of a bewigged footman for Viceroy's House, New Delhi.*

with which the chair was covered lasted for fifty-odd years in spite of constant use and never had to be professionally cleaned – it was merely sponged.

Lutyens designed many light fittings. In his houses, he often favoured glazed star lanterns, particularly as pendants in circulation areas. His billiard table light fitting with its individual conical shades, for Marshcourt, was another fine example of his work in this area. When designing fittings for electrical light, he responded to the relatively new technology in an essentially imaginative and modern way.

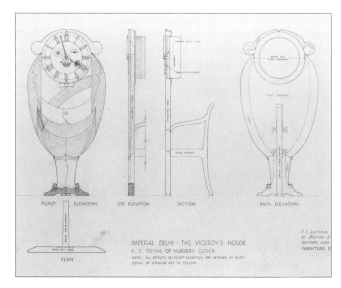

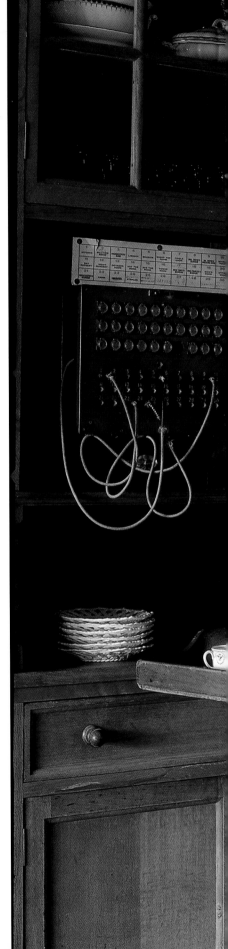

Somehow Lutyens also found time to design clocks. Mary Lutyens describes what she believed to be his most ingenious, one of the clocks specially made for New Delhi: 'The case is of wood, gracefully shaped like an urn with two brass handles, painted pale blue and standing about 1½ feet high, the face of a horizontal oval, the hands expanding like lazy tongs to reach their fullest extent at the figures nine and three.' The brass key is in the form of a pansy (*pensée*) – a reminder to wind the clock.

ABOVE: Detail of chest at Midland Bank, Poultry, designed for the storage of the bankers' top hats.

RIGHT: The room call indicator and telephone exchange in the pantry at Castle Drogo.

Viceroy's House, which had occupied so much of his productive life, called forth some of his finest work in all spheres. It is small wonder that when the house was formally opened and the time came for Lutyens to hand it over, he was lost for words. 'I had not the nerve to say goodbye to Irwin [the Viceroy],' said Lutyens. 'I just walked out and kissed a wall of the House.'

DELIGHT

Lutyens's houses echoed, in his words, with the 'rhythms familiar in human life'. Their spatial poetry, of movement, surprise and arrival gave them animation and personality. The solidity and craftsmanship of their construction provided a rooted sense of security and continuity. On the level of detail and practicality, they expressed a domestic ideal. They were, in short, full of delight.

Delight permeates Lutyens's work. Little is repeated, little is to order, little is merely driven by function or purpose. But delight is also present in a more obvious sense, as the natural irrepressible expression of a personality with a great sense of fun. A typical *jeu d'esprit* can be found at Orchards above the fireplace in the study, where a plan of the house was painted directly on to the tiled surround. Another takes the form of a movable garden seat. A slatted high-backed garden seat with scrolled arms is one of Lutyens's more familiar furniture designs; in the version made for Ednaston Manor, handles protrude from one end of the bench, while the other is fitted with a large wheel: half bench, half wheelbarrow. At the house where Lutyens spent his later

RIGHT: One of Lutyens's best-known furniture designs is this scrolled-back garden seat, which he used in many of his gardens.

ABOVE: *Designed for Ednaston Manor, this high-backed garden seat features handles at one end and a wheel at the other – half-bench, half-wheelbarrow – a characteristic Lutyens joke.*

years working on New Delhi, No I. Bungalow, Mary Lutyens remembers her father having a blackboard top made to cover the dining table. Supplied with chalk, even the shyest guests soon amused themselves with games of noughts and crosses.

BELOW: Toy theatre in Queen Mary's Dolls' House. Lutyens designed the original sets for Peter Pan.

But it was in the design of nursery fittings and furniture that Lutyens's sense of play found freest rein.

The nursery was a big square room, with a gay frieze round the walls of nursery tale pictures and jungle animals. There was a bathroom leading out of it, and the playroom was next door. The window to which the strange boy had come had

never had bars across as most nurseries do. Wendy's bed was nearest the fire, which had a brass fireguard set round it. The boys were on the other side of the room, and over each bed was a night light, fixed to the wall ...

wrote J.M. Barrie, Lutyens's friend, describing the Darling children's night nursery in *Peter Pan,* which was supposedly modelled on the Lutyens children's nursery at Bloomsbury Square.

There is a story that Lutyens was asked if it was true that he had once designed a circular nursery, to which he replied that he had. When asked why, he answered that it was so that no child could ever be sent to stand in the corner. Whether or not this story is apocryphal, Lutyens's great affinity with children and his ability to see the fun in things resulted in some of his most charming and witty designs. In two of his English country houses, there were windows at low level in the nurseries so that toddlers and

ABOVE: *Day Nursery from Queen Mary's Dolls'
House. Lutyens particularly loved designing for
children, with whom he had a special rapport.*

crawling children could look out. At the British
Embassy in Washington, he provided another special
vantage point, a small window in the main staircase
so that the children on the nursery floor could look
down at arriving guests.

Predictably, perhaps, it was New Delhi which
offered the greatest scope for his playful ideas. The
floor of the nursery in the Viceroy's residence was
patterned with large red and white checks for games
of chess, backgammon or draughts. The nursery
gallery was grouped round an internal court, but for
safety's sake the opening had to be fitted with a
screen. Lutyens built a huge bird cage into each side
of this screen, for colourful parrots to dispel any
hint of confinement.

Lutyens's punning nature expressed itself in tor-

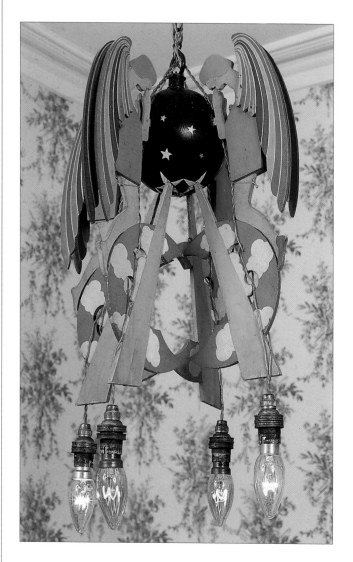

chandeliers for the nursery at New Delhi. Made out of painted wood, one is in the form of four prancing ponies; another shows four angels praying; another depicts boys fishing among bullrushes: the light bulbs are at the end of the fishing rods, while fish curl round to bite them. But the most ingenious comprises four hens and chicks. Hanging from the branches of the fitting are broken egg shells, from which spill the bulbs – the 'yolks'.

LEFT: *One of the electric chandeliers designed for the nursery at Viceroy's House, New Delhi. Made out of painted wood, this one shows four angels kneeling in prayer.*

BELOW: *One of Lutyens's wittiest designs: a light fitting featuring hens and chicks. Hanging from the branches of the fitting are broken egg shells spilling out the lightbulbs – the 'yolks/jokes'.*

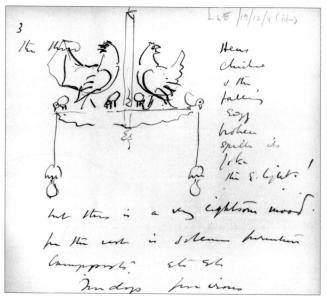

rents of visual jokes. On the long sea voyages to India, he amused himself by converting the letter-head of the P&O line into fanciful pictorial doodles – 'two people in one cabin trying to put on the same shirt', 'the tiger is an awful beast', 'the jolly sisters' … He delighted in producing comic drawings for children. 'Lays Majesty' depicts a giant hen laying an egg, out of which hatches a little figure. Similar trains of thought inspired the designs of electric

ABOVE: *Fishing boys animate this electric chandelier, designed for the nursery at Viceroy's House, New Delhi. The lightbulbs are suspended from the wooden frame.*

RIGHT: *Shipboard doodle: 'The tiger is an awful beast'. Lutyens made scores of these comic sketches incorporating the letterhead of the P&O line.*

Writing in the *New York Times*, Ada Louise Huxtable declared that 'Lutyens is exactly the sort of architect to intrigue us ... Today's architects, lovers of learned paradox, find his work full of marvellous visual ambiguities and erudite references. He is an architect of flux and surprise, wit, anticlimax, ambiguity and sheer delight.' Delight was the way in which Lutyens wore his immense architectural learning lightly.

SELECT BIBLIOGRAPHY

Brown, Jane, *Lutyens and the Edwardians: An English Architect and his Clients,* Viking, 1996

Butler, A.S.G. with George Stuart and Christopher Hussey *The Architecture of Sir Edwin Lutyens,* three volumes, *Country Life,* 1950

Gradidge, Roderick, *Edwin Lutyens, Architect Laureate,* George Allen & Unwin, 1981

Hussey, Christopher, *Life of Lutyens,* Country Life, 1950

Inskip, Peter, *Edwin Lutyens,* Academy Editions, 1979

Irving, R.G. *Indian Summer,* Yale, 1981

Jekyll, Gertrude, *Home and Garden,* London, 1900

Lutyens, *The Work of the English Architect Sir Edwin Lutyens (1869–1944),* Arts Council of Great Britain, 1982

Lutyens, Mary, *Edwin Lutyens: A Memoir,* Murray, 1980

Lutyens, Robert, *Six Great Architects,* London, 1959

Percy, Clayre and Ridley, Jane, *Letters of Edwin Lutyens,* Collins, 1985

Richardson, Margaret, *Catalogue of the Drawings Collection of the Royal Institute of British Architects: Lutyens,* Farnborough, 1973

Rollo, John, '*Metiendo Vivendum*: "By Measure We Must Live" ', *Architectural Research Quarterly,* vol. 3, no. 2, 1999

Weaver, Lawrence, 'Houses and Gardens by E. L. Lutyens', *Country Life,* 1913; Antique Collector's Club, 1981

USEFUL ADDRESSES

THE LUTYENS TRUST

Lutyens's buildings, particularly his houses, are of a size and type which has made them particularly vulnerable. The fact that so many have survived is due to the efforts of such groups as The Lutyens Trust, Registered Charity No: 326776, an organisation whose members are dedicated to conserving Lutyens's buildings and preserving the spirit of his designs. In addition, the Trust provides information on all aspects of Lutyens's life and career and publishes a regular newsletter. For further information, for membership enquiries, donations and subscriptions, tel: 01306 730487.

THE NATIONAL TRUST
36 Queen Anne's Gate
London SW1H 9AS
tel: 020 7222 9251
for membership contact:
National Trust Membership Department
PO Box 39
Bromley
Kent BR1 3XL
tel: 020 8315 1111

NATIONAL GARDENS SCHEME
Some Lutyens gardens are open occasionally under the National Gardens scheme. Contact tel: 01483 211535 for details.

LUTYENS DESIGN ASSOCIATES
Lutyens furniture made to order from the original drawings. Pieces include chairs, sofas, dining tables, occasional tables and console tables.
tel: 020 8780 5977
website: www.lutyens-furniture.com

PLACES TO VISIT

Few of Lutyens's houses are open to the public. Those that may be visited, rather than merely glimpsed from the roadside, include the following:

SURREY
GODDARDS, Abinger. Administered by the Landmark Trust. Public visits on Wednesday afternoons can be arranged by prior appointment.
(tel: 01306 730871)

MUNSTEAD WOOD, near Milford. The garden is open to visitors occasionally under the National Gardens Scheme.

GODALMING MUSEUM, Godalming. Collection contains items items relating to Jekyll.
(tel: 01483 426 510)

SUSSEX
LITTLE THAKEHAM, Storrington. Now run as a country house hotel.
(tel: 01903 744416)

SOMERSET
HESTERCOMBE, near Taunton. Garden open every day from May to September.

DEVON
CASTLE DROGO, Drewsteignton, nr Exeter. Owned by the National Trust and open April to October, daily except Fridays.

KENT
GREAT DIXTER, Northiam. Garden (by Christopher Lloyd) and house open every day except Mondays from April to October.

BERKSHIRE
FOLLY FARM, Sulhamstead. Garden open occasionally under the National Gardens Scheme.

WINDSOR CASTLE, Windsor. The Queen Mary's Dolls' House is on permanent display. The tomb of King George V and Queen Mary in St George's Chapel was designed by Lutyens.

HERTFORDSHIRE
KNEBWORTH HOUSE, Stevenage. Garden and house open to the public, April to September; daily during the Easter holidays and from July to September, weekends at other times.

NORTHUMBERLAND
LINDISFARNE CASTLE, Holy Island. Owned by the National Trust and open April to October, daily except for Fridays.

SCOTLAND
GREY WALLS, Guillane, near Edinburgh. Now run as a country house hotel.
(tel: 01620 842144)

FRANCE
LES BOIS DES MOUTIERS, Varengeville, Normandy. Garden open in the summer months.

INDEX

AUTHOR'S ACKNOWLEDGEMENTS

I must thank, first of all, Candia Lutyens and Paul Peterson of Lutyens Design Associates for their generous support and encouragement. Candia Lutyens contributed the Foreword, read the manuscript and gave permission for me to quote from an unpublished memoir written by her father, Robert Lutyens. Paul Peterson provided much welcome assistance with respect to sources, both written and visual.

I am particularly grateful to Clayre Percy and Jane Brown, acknowledged experts on the life and work of Lutyens, for reading the manuscript in draft form. Their comments were invaluable. Michael and Frances Edwards pointed out many relevant themes and details of Lutyens's domestic architecture.

At Pavilion, thanks are due to Colin Webb, Vivien James, Clare Johnson and Morwenna Wallis. Special thanks to Jenny de Gex, whose sterling efforts vastly exceeded the brief of picture research and to James Mortimer for original photography in difficult circumstances.

PICTURE ACKNOWLEDGEMENTS

Special photography by James Mortimer by kind permission of the individual property owners 12, 54-55, 59, 61, 62-63, 64, 64-65, 68, 70, 71, 76, 77, 87, 88, 89, 97, 100-101, 106-107, 108-109, 120, 121, 122, 138-139, 143, 146-147, 148-149, 150, 151, 152-153, 154 TL, 154-155, 173, 176

Arcaid/Richard Bryant 11, 73, 102, 103

Arcaid/Lucinda Lambton 66

Jane Brown/courtesy Jekyll Family Trust 105

Jane Brown/courtesy Geoffrey Robinson 25

Christie's Images 158-159, 174L

Country Life 10, 15, 21, 36, 43, 44-45, 74, 75, 91, 92-93, 94, 110, 126, 127, 137, 140, 142, 180

Country Life/Jonathan Gibson 2, 26-27, 79, 98-99

Country Life/ Alex Starkey 33

Frances and Michael Edwards, Architects 29

By kind permission of the Godalming Museum Shop 178-179

Hulton Getty 51

Interior Archive/Christopher Simon Sykes 111

Interior Archive/Fritz von der Schulenburg 112, 113, 114

Knebworth House Collection 124, 125

Candia Lutyens 8, 19, 50

Lutyens Design Associates 35, 52, 57, 144-145, 167, 171

James Mortimer Archive 84-85, 130-131, 134, 168-169, 172, 175

National Trust Photo Library/Joe Cornish 30-31

National Trust Photo Library/Chris Gascoigne 39

National Trust Photo Library/James Mortimer 90, 118-119, 176-177

National Trust Photo Library /Andreas von Einsiedel 83, 117, 129, 133, 162, 164-165

National Trust Photo Library/ Charlie Waite 80-81

Private Collection/ photo Angelo Hornak 23

Private Collection/photo Eddie Ryle-Hodges 184L, 185T

Courtesy Jane Ridley 49

British Architectural Library/RIBA, London 5, 20, 67, 156, 158, 168, 170L, 170R, 174R, 184R, 185B

The Royal Collection(c) 2000, Her Majesty Queen Elizabeth II 181, 182-183

Sotheby's 157

NA
997
L8
W55
2000

Wilhide, Elizabeth.

Sir Edwin Lutyens.

$39.95

DATE			

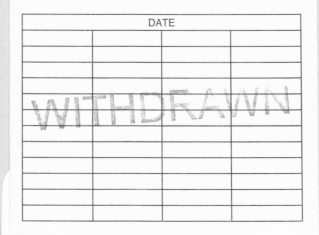

NA
997
L8

CARROLL COMMUNITY COLLEGE LMTS

Sir Edwin Lutyens.

00000009375346

Learning Resources Center
Carroll Community College
1601 Washington Rd.
Westminster, MD 21157

APR 0 4 2001

BAKER & TAYLOR